THE CHOLESTEROL CLEAN-OUT™

By
Peter Cox and Peggy Brusseau

Published by Century Hutchinson Ltd
Brookmount House, 62-65 Chandos Place, Covent Garden,
London WC2N 4NW

Century Hutchinson Australia (Pty) Ltd
88-91 Albion Street, Surry Hills, NSW 2010, Australia

Century Hutchinson New Zealand Ltd
PO Box 40-086, 32-34 View Road, Glenfield, Auckland 10,
New Zealand

Century Hutchinson South Africa (Pty) Ltd,
PO Box 337, Bergvlei, 2012, South Africa

First published in 1989

Set in Century Schoolbook by SX Composing Ltd
22 Sirdar Road, Rayleigh, Essex.

Printed and bound in by The Guernsey Press,
Guernsey, Channel Islands

British Library Cataloguing in Publication Data
Cox, Peter, 1955-
  The Quick Cholesterol Clean-Out
  1, Man. Cholesterol. Control. Diet
  I. Title II. Brusseau, Peggy
  616.1'05

  ISBN 0-7126-3087-2

CONTENTS

ACKNOWLEDGEMENTS

We would like to thank everyone who has so kindly given their time and shared their expertise with us on this project. Carol Bateman SRD, Dr Denis Burkitt, Professor Michael Crawford, Professor Barry Lewis, Dr Bruce Middleton and Dr D A T Southgate all generously helped us to understand aspects of this cholesterol business. Most of all, we would like to express our appreciation to the intrepid band of volunteers who so willingly tested our diets and made so many useful suggestions.

PDC
MAB

IMPORTANT NOTE

The recommendations made in this book are for adults only. If you suspect you may suffer from a raised cholesterol level, we strongly advise you to seek qualified medical treatment. Do not attempt self-treatment without first discussing and agreeing the proposed treatment with your doctor. Diagnosis and treatment of medical conditions is a responsibility shared between you and your doctor and neither the authors nor publisher can accept responsibility for the consequences of treatment based on the recommendations described herein.

Back cover photograph by Carole Latimer.

INTRODUCTION

Before you begin, the good news. . . . We've written this book to bring you this most urgent message: *You can take simple steps right now to significantly reduce the level of cholesterol in your blood, and so greatly cut your risk of suffering a stroke or heart attack.*

You've probably heard that too much cholesterol in the blood is a bad thing. Cholesterol builds up on your artery walls, causing the artery-narrowing disease called atherosclerosis, which is the leading cause of heart attacks and strokes.

You may also know that eating the wrong foods can contribute to an unhealthily high level of cholesterol. But did you know that you can actually reduce your cholesterol count without resorting to a lifetime's dependency on powerful drugs and strict medication?

The fact is, you can.

Not enough people know this yet. Nonetheless, the evidence is steadily mounting all the time – as you'll see. Researchers all round the world are reporting the same findings, that a high cholesterol level can be conquered – if you're willing to try. The proof is coming in all the time. In a recent issue of the *Journal of the American Medical Association* researchers reported that people could lower their cholesterol levels just as effectively by eating a cup and a half of oat bran every day as they could by taking expensive drugs – at a fraction of the cost! 'If you can do it with diet, why use drugs?' says researcher Dr Bruce Kinosian, a professor of medicine at the University of Maryland in Baltimore. Why indeed?

In this book, we've assembled the latest evidence to show you how you can take simple steps to reduce your risk of suffering from the consequences of a high cholesterol level.

Although *The Quick Cholesterol Clean-Out* includes diets and other natural ways of lowering cholesterol, we wouldn't want you to think that a wonderful cholesterol level is the *only* ingredient of a healthy way of living. So please read – and make sure you act upon – the other simple lifestyle improvements we suggest. We are convinced that, taken together, the techniques explained in this book can save many thousands of lives.

PETER COX
PEGGY BRUSSEAU
London, 1989

1
YOU *CAN* SAVE YOUR LIFE!

Every day of your life, your body produces about one gram of a pearl-like, fatty substance called cholesterol. Why you should produce so much is a deep mystery because, although you need some cholesterol in your system to make hormones, bile and cell membranes, this essential requirement only comes to about one-third of your body's total daily production.

Most of this never-ending cholesterol output takes place inside your liver, synthesized by a couple of dozen different enzymes. However – and just think about this – *almost every cell in your body* has the capacity to make cholesterol for itself.

Can you imagine? Countless millions of busy little cholesterol factories situated throughout your entire body, each one of them ready to manufacture cholesterol on-site. It's almost as if your body was expecting a global cholesterol shortage at any moment . . . except, of course, that in today's world there is *never* likely to be a cholesterol shortage – in fact, quite the opposite. Because on top of the one gram your body produces internally, you also take in about half a gram of cholesterol every day from your diet, in the form of animal foods.

The fact is that, every day, your body will produce and take in about *four times* as much cholesterol as you actually need. And although some of it will be processed into hormones, some will be used to make cell membranes, and some will be excreted, a little will probably stick around in your system, slowly building up year by year, until eventually the level of cholesterol in your blood may become dangerously high.

But by then, the damage could well have been done.

THE CHOLESTEROL TIMEBOMB

Because it happens so slowly, you don't notice it. No-one can *feel* their cholesterol level as it builds up, and even when an artery becomes more than half blocked by this fatty, cholesterol-rich sludge known as 'atheroma', you still may not be aware of any warning signs to tell you that something is badly wrong. In fact, an artery usually has to be more than 75 per cent blocked before blood flow is seriously impeded. But by this stage, time is definitely running out. Our bodies depend on the normal flow of blood through minute capillaries, larger arteries (which transport oxygen-rich blood away from the heart) and veins (which carry blood back to the heart again) to nourish all our organs and body tissues, and this same remarkable system, consisting of thousands of kilometres of blood vessels, also helps to eliminate waste products. Every day, your heart will beat 100,000 times (2,500 million times in a lifetime) as it provides the motive power to drive this huge network of intricately connected blood vessels. Every minute, your heart circulates your body's entire volume of blood, about 5 litres, once round your system (pumping 200 million litres in a lifetime). If your heart stops beating for more than 3 minutes, permanent brain damage may occur. Being a hard-working muscle, the heart also supplies itself with vital oxygen and nourishment through its own pumping actions and again, if the blood flow through the life-giving coronary arteries is stopped for more than a few minutes, the heart will be damaged to such a great extent that it may be irreversibly stopped. So you see, with such a complex circulatory system, when something happens to interrupt or diminish your blood flow, the situation can become very serious, very quickly.

As cholesterol builds up on the walls of the arteries, the passages begin to narrow. If allowed to continue, this process will ultimately deprive vital organs of their blood supply, and you will die. But don't make the mistake of thinking that a high cholesterol level in your blood is associated only with heart disease. In fact, the same cholesterol which forms deposits that build up on artery walls can also act to reduce the flow of blood causing what we commonly know as a 'stroke'. Most strokes are caused by a narrowing or blockage of an artery, leading to a 'cerebrovascular accident', involving damage to the brain. Of course, those who survive a heart attack or stroke *can* make a good recovery, if they are prepared to change their lifestyles sufficiently. But wouldn't it be more sensible to take *preventative* action now, rather than fighting for your life later on?

WHEN HEARTS BREAK

You will probably be surprised to learn that the very first clear, clinical account of someone having a heart attack was written only as recently as 1912. Until then, it seems as if heart attacks were so rare they just weren't recorded. Today, of course, heart disease is the commonest cause of death in the Western world. This means that heart disease is an *epidemic of the twentieth century*. It means that over the past 80 years, something has happened to make a once rare and unusual form of death so common that by the age of 65, one man out of every five has had a heart attack, and of those, one in ten has died. Although two-thirds of heart attacks happen to men, this still means that, in the United States for example, about 400,000 women have a heart attack every year. Heart disease is now so common that most of us have had a traumatic encounter with it, in one form or another. Here is one personal account from Peter, co-author of this book.

'I was still a teenager when my dad died from a heart attack. It's a painful and vivid memory that I don't think I'll ever be able to wipe from my mind. It was just past midnight, and my family was turning in for the night. We'd all said goodnight to each other, and my parents had gone upstairs to bed. Then I remember a scream from my mother – I'd never in my life heard such an alarming and heartbreaking sound. I rushed upstairs, and my father was clutching at his chest, he couldn't speak, he was trying desperately to breathe. We got him on to the bed, and I tried resuscitation, but it just didn't work. I phoned a doctor and kept on trying to breathe life into him, but I eventually had to accept that my father was quite dead. My mother was shattered. She kept calling his name. It haunts me still.

'Our doctor told us that there was nothing else we could have done, that his heart attack was so massive that no-one could have saved him. But even so, you blame yourself. You wonder if you could have done something else, anything, to keep him alive.

'The thing about a heart attack is that it seems so sudden and utterly devastating. It's as if the body has instantaneously switched off all life-support systems – as if it has decided that it simply wants to die. But in reality, a heart attack is just the traumatic culmination of a long process of degeneration which started many years before. I saw this for myself when, some time after my father's death, I found myself standing in a London teaching hospital, preparing to inspect a diseased heart that had been taken from someone who had died from a coronary.

'If you've never seen a human heart, you'd be surprised first of all by the size of it, particularly a diseased one. It's a good deal bigger than the small and neat pump-like organ you might be expecting. One of the arteries had been cut open to show a cross-section through it. It was nearly blocked by atheroma – the name they give to the yellowish, porridge-like substance that builds up inside arteries and eventually blocks them. It reminded me of a kitchen kettle that had become completely clogged up with limescale. Then – and this was the most unpleasant part for me personally – you could see where a truly massive haemorrhage had occurred. This person's life had been ended by a final, fatal blockage in an artery, leading to a haemorrhage which left the bottom half of the heart completely soaked in blood. Just like my father, there was nothing kind or gentle about the way this person had died.'

GETTING VALUE FROM LIFE

This book has a positive message. It's about living life to the fullest, and about out-smarting the Grim Reaper as much as possible, for as long as possible. You've undoubtedly heard people say things like: 'You can't live for ever', 'you've got to die of something', and similar remarks intended to lower their own expectations (and yours too) of ever reaching a happy old age. Well, people like that wouldn't have got very far with Shigechiyo Izumi, who died in 1986 at the ludicrous (by our standards) age of 120. That's *twice* as long as many people in the West live. This remarkable, yet unassuming, man lived in southern Japan, and was born there when his country was still ruled by a war-lord *shogun*. He made his living as a farmer, and his appetite for life, and indeed his appetite for the opposite sex, was undimmed right up to his long-delayed passing. You may be wondering what sort of diet he ate. Well, in some important ways it was similar to the diets contained in this book.

So why *shouldn't* you raise your lifetime expectations at this very moment? Can you think of any good reasons why, for example, you shouldn't set yourself a three-figure target to aim for? One hundred is a nice, round number, isn't it!

Let's answer one more question which may be in your mind at this stage – and it's a key question. '*Is it worth it? If I reduce my blood cholesterol level, does it mean that I'll be immune to heart attacks and coronary heart disease?*'

We'll try to answer this as honestly and completely as science will currently allow us to. First, no-one can *guarantee* that reducing your cholesterol level will prevent you suffering from heart disease. Life is just not like that. There is no such thing as *absolute* certainty. The man who smokes 60 cigarettes a day *may* just live to be seventy (although the odds are heavily against it). If you try to walk across a busy road wearing a blindfold over your eyes you *may* just reach the other side in one piece. If you play Russian roulette with a loaded gun, you *may* just get lucky and not blow your brains out.

But come on – let's be sensible. Life is already risky enough and full enough of surprises (some of them rather nasty) for us to know that some chances are much riskier than others. Only a fool, an addicted gambler or someone with a death-wish would knowingly take a risk which is overwhelmingly likely to end in their own fatality. And yet, that's precisely what you're doing if you maintain a high blood cholesterol level and do nothing about it. The odds are against you. Massively. And even if you like to live dangerously (maybe you're one of those people who thrives on danger, adventure and the smell of catastrophe in your nostrils), why not take up mountain-climbing, parachuting or hang-gliding instead? You'll certainly get more pleasure out of them, and if you reduce your cholesterol level as well, you may stick around a little longer to enjoy them!

When we set out to write this book, we decided to keep it simple and to avoid as many unnecessary figures, percentages, and mathematical calculations as we could, but there is one fundamental little formula which is so important that we're including it right now. It is, indeed, *so* important that you should memorize it. Here it is: ***For every 1 per cent drop in blood cholesterol, there is a 2 per cent drop in the risk of cardiovascular disease.***

Think about this for a moment. It means that when a population manages to reduce its cholesterol level by – say – a meagre 5 per cent, the risk of cardiovascular disease drops by 10 per cent. And if the level of cholesterol declines by 10 per cent, then the risk drops by 20 per cent. And so on. Now of course, this fact has profound implications for all of us. It means that reducing our blood cholesterol level is one of the most effective ways yet discovered to *dramatically reduce* our risk of suffering from – or being killed by – cardiovascular disease.

There is hard proof of this statement. Since 1960, Americans have on average lowered their cholesterol levels by 3 to 4 per cent – which may not sound very much, until you learn that death rates from heart disease dropped from 286 deaths per 100,000 population in 1960 to 180 per 100,000 in 1985 – actually a reduction of 37 per cent! 'This is the most dramatic trend in death rates in the world', says Dr Patrick L. Remington of the Center for Disease Control. 'The eyes of the entire world's scientific community are on the United States because deaths from heart disease are going down so rapidly.' How has such a change been achieved? Dr Remington believes that about half the decline in coronary deaths can be attributed to changes in lifestyle, and about a third due to changes in the diet, including the consumption of foods which are beneficial to blood cholesterol levels.

Although the American experience is clearly encouraging and shows the rest of the world just what can be achieved, there is still much more to do. For example, only one out of every ten Americans actually knows what their current cholesterol level is. Do *you* know?

LOW-RISK LIVING

Dr Remington spoke about 'changes in lifestyle' managing to achieve an enormous reduction in deaths. What does this mean? Well, it means that cardiovascular disease is the result of an inter-play of factors – of which a high cholesterol level is an important (but not the only) one. So what are the others?

Smoking

Stub it out, before it stubs you out. According to Professor Julian Peto of the Institute of Cancer Research the only thing that persuades more than 50 per cent of smokers to give up is having a heart attack. So get ahead of the game and stop while you're ahead. Better still, don't start.

High blood pressure

Get your blood pressure checked. Cut down on the salt you eat, lose weight, and cut down on alcohol. And learn how to relax – stress can be a killer.

Obesity

A high blood cholesterol level occurs more than twice as often in the overweight than in the non-overweight . . . even 5 ex-cess pounds can threaten your health. Try pinching the skin under your upper arm. Slightly more than 1 inch (2.5 cm) thickness of skin is acceptable for a man, slightly less than that for a woman. More than this, and you may need to lose weight.

Lack of exercise

Studies show that women who don't exercise are three times more likely to die of a heart attack than those who stay in shape. Exercise combined with dieting may be the most effec-tive way to lose weight and keep it off, and protects against heart disease.

In Chapter Six, we'll consider how you can modify these other risk factors to produce a low-risk lifestyle. But for the moment, let's just remember that by focussing on cholesterol, we're not implying that it is the *only* consideration. A man who manages to lower his blood cholesterol while still smoking 60 cigarettes a day might just as well not have bothered. So examine the other risk factors in your life, and take corrective action where necessary.

GENETIC FACTORS

Sometimes we hear about a 'genetic' factor in heart disease – that people with a history of heart disease in the family are more likely to contract heart disease themselves. Scientific evidence shows that this is true, and doctors have termed this inherited high level of blood cholesterol as 'familial hypercholesterolaemia' or FH for short. However, it would be a great mistake to assume that either you are 'doomed' to suffer from heart disease simply because one member of your family has suffered from it, or, alternatively, that you will miraculously escape it because no close relative has succumbed. Here are some important points to bear in mind:

● Firstly, FH is not a diagnosis you can make for yourself. Just because a relative has died from heart disease doesn't mean that you have FH.
● Secondly, only one in 500 people has FH, whereas one in every five people has an excessively high level of blood cholesterol, and *two-thirds* of the population should modify their diet, according to Professor Barry Lewis, a leading authority.[1]
● Thirdly, if you do have a history of heart disease in your family, it is even more important that you take steps – including dietary ones – to reduce your cholesterol level.
● And lastly, we went to visit a top specialist who treats hundreds of people with high blood cholesterol every year, and asked him how many of his patients' high blood cholesterol was caused by genetic reasons. 'Very few,' he said. 'The vast majority are as a result of years of inappropriate diet.' Get the message?

CONFUSED? YOU'RE MEANT TO BE

Every so often, almost as regular as clockwork, a maverick doctor or 'diet guru' will appear and receive massive publicity for their peculiar views about cholesterol and heart disease. The reason that they receive such a huge amount of publicity is that their opinions – for that is all they are, they are rarely supported by facts – are so way out of line with almost every other professional that the news media is enthralled. The message that these heretics bring to us is usually the same – 'Eat as much junk food as you want to, don't worry about cutting down on fat in your diet, there is no connection between diet and heart disease.' One such doctor surfaced recently in the United States, where he was widely quoted as saying: 'There's more nutrition in a candy bar than in an apple'; 'There is no correlation between cholesterol in the diet and cholesterol in your blood'; 'Chances are that sugar won't kill you and neither will fats'; and 'A heavy hand with the salt-shaker won't do most of us any harm at all.' We won't name this doctor, because he's already received enough publicity without our help (he was, of course, promoting his new diet book at the time). In Britain, too, another doctor – by a strange coincidence also promoting *his* own diet book – recently came out with the same type of headline-grabbing conclusions, saying 'Food is not an important or a modifiable cause of disease in our society.' This same doctor also became an adviser to a television series in which his own views received much prominence.

To *real* medical specialists in the field (some of these diet-gurus are often little more than general practitioners with little real knowledge of the subject), it must be dispiriting in the extreme to hear such damaging opinions given the full weight and support of media attention. After all, when the public sees a doctor publicly state on television that 'food is not a cause of disease', many people will think twice before they change their diets for the better (why bother?), and many more will simply become confused and do nothing to change bad eating habits that may send them to an early grave. We spoke to one eminent authority on the metabolism of fats, Professor Michael Crawford, a man who has spent much of his life exploring the connection between diet and disease. We asked him what he thought about the television doctor who believed that food is not a cause of disease. 'The fact of the matter is that it is not a tenable position,' he said. 'You must consider the evidence. Right from the very beginning, from his very first words, this man exposes his total ignorance about the relationship between food and disease.'

'How do you feel about the amount of publicity views such as his receive?' we asked. 'Well,' he replied, 'I suppose anybody can get up and write a book saying that the earth's not round, it's flat, and they will get enormous publicity.'

A rather more obscure source of 'disinformation' comes from certain quarters within the food industry. In Britain, for example, the meat industry mounted a publicity campaign starring one of the world's top nutritionists, who was featured in consumer brochures saying that there was no 'conclusive proof' of the relationship between animal fat consumption and heart disease. Nowhere, however, was it pointed out to the public that this nutritionist was actually being *paid* by the meat industry to advance their case, and persuade people to go on buying their products. Even in schools, children have been bombarded by the most misleading publicity from sausage and pork pie manufacturers, which gives the impression that their products are a 'health food', while cunningly avoiding even mentioning the word 'fat' once. Indeed, it appears that there is a large and well-funded lobby whose object is to *stop* the public receiving timely advice about beneficial changes to their diet. 'After I appeared on a television station,' writes one doctor, 'and gave my opinion that a high fat diet containing too much butter and milk could lead to heart disease, the Head of Features at the television station received a letter from the chief executive of a butter industry lobby group. After commenting on my remarks about butter, he wrote: "*On the day that this was transmitted we were about to commit to a burst of advertising on your station. I think that you can probably well imagine that this decision came under review in the light of such remarks*".' It takes a brave television station or newspaper, doesn't it, to stand up to pressure like this?

In the face of such pressure, propaganda and arm-twisting by various self-interested persons and lobbies, surely, you might think, our governments should take steps to look after our health. Well, don't depend on it. 'Healthy eating' is a subject which is rarely out of the news these days, and in Britain, as in many other countries, the government has made public statements about the need for us all to eat a better diet. One of the ministers responsible for the nation's health said that very often the problem for people was just ignorance and failing to realize that they do have some control over their lives. Some of those problems could be tackled by impressing on people the need to look after themselves better, then society would end up with better health for everyone. The substance of the minister's comment was that 'health care' is what you get when things go wrong in society, but that in most advanced societies, people are taking much more interest in making sure that as far as possible things don't go wrong.

The message is clear – don't expect 'the government' (whoever it happens to be) to assume responsibility for your own health. In fact, some health experts believe the governments have a vested interest in keeping people in a state of *sickness*. Incredible? Listen to one doctor:

'The plain, undeniable truth is that not even the Government wants us to know how to stay healthy. Every year the British treasury receives over £9,000 million from the tobacco and alcohol industries alone. Without that money coming in income tax would have to rise to politically unacceptable levels.'[2]

This same person – Dr Vernon Coleman, a well-known medical writer – believes that there is a further reason for a general lack of interest in widespread preventive medicine:

'In Britain – as elsewhere in the developed world – workers who are currently paying pension contributions assume that the money they are paying will be invested and repaid to them when they reach pensionable age. That is not the case. The state pension contributions paid by today's workers are used to pay the pensions of yesterday's workers – today's pensioners. The state pensions that today's workers will receive when they retire will be paid by the regular contributions made by tomorrow's workers. It doesn't take much imagination to see the sort of problems that are likely to arise ... politicians are very well aware that if we cut the number of people dying from heart disease and cancer then our economic position will be even more precarious than it is at the moment.'[3]

Politically, then, it *just could be* that our governments don't want us to live to a ripe old age. Which means, more than ever, that we all must look after ourselves better, because if we don't, no-one else is going to.

WHAT'S GONE WRONG?

Since 1912, when the first ever medical observation was made of a heart attack, heart disease has soared to become the number one killer of our civilization. But why? What has changed in such a short space of time? We asked Professor Crawford:

'What has happened is that we all started from a common baseline of wild foods. This is the sort of "primitive" diet which humans have eaten throughout most of their evolution, over the past five million years. However, in the last few centuries, things have gone haywire. In Europe, our diets have gone in one direction, in Africa and India they've gone in a different direction. In western Europe we've focussed on consuming foods which are very rich in non-essential types of fat, but pretty miserable sources of essential fats. Our diets have also become rich in processed and refined carbohydrates. In fact, the problems are quite easy to identify – it's taking corrective action that seems to be difficult for some of us.'

So what is this 'primitive' diet, and how does it differ from the one which most of us eat today? Some fascinating research holds the key. Human genetics have changed very little over the past 40,000 years (barely a tick of the evolutionary clock), but our diets *have* changed – and mostly, they've changed radically over the past century or two. When scientists set out to discover what sort of diet we are 'genetically programmed' to eat, they found that there were tremendous differences between today's highly processed food and our 'original' diet. Using evidence gathered from fossilized remains, and also studying the feeding patterns of modern-day hunter-gatherer tribes, they found that there were indeed great differences between our 'original' diet and the one that most of us in the West eat today. In fact, they coined a new phrase to describe the composition of today's food – 'affluent malnutrition'. This doesn't refer to the type of malnutrition evident during famines (which is first and foremost a lack of *any* food, basically a lack of calories), but to an overall imbalance of the diet, involving too much of the wrong sorts of nutrients, and not enough of the right ones.

The chart that follows shows some of the main changes which have occurred. You can see that although the amount of cholesterol directly consumed in our food has more or less stayed the same, the amount of fat in our diets has soared, in fact doubled. While the amount of protein has approximately halved, sodium (salt) has increased by a factor of six, but the essential nutrients of calcium, vitamin C and fibre have all plunged drastically. One further, and very significant, point is that it's not just that the overall amount of fat has doubled, the *type* of fat has changed tremendously, too. Very little saturated fat was consumed 40,000 years ago, since most dietary fats were either mono-unsaturated or polyunsaturated. All in all, it seems as if the human race has unwittingly been playing a huge experiment on itself over the past 100 or so years, since the Industrial Revolution started to fundamentally change – and apparently impoverish – our diets. In the year 1860, about one-quarter of our energy came from fat sources. By 1910, this had risen to one-third, and by 1975 about 45 per cent of our total energy intake was coming from fat. Thus, in just over a century, the amount of fat in our diet has doubled. So it's hardly surprising if this *new* diet which we're eating today has some rather dreadful side-effects, in the form of diet-related diseases.

How Our Diet has Changed Since The Stone-Age

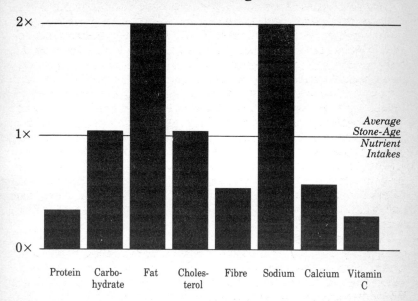

WHAT ARE YOUR OPTIONS?

If you have a high cholesterol level, you can do one of three things. One option is to do nothing. This is what most people do at the moment, and it's one of the reasons why the cost of heart and other related diseases is so appallingly high. Another option is to take dietary steps to reduce it. That's why this book was written – and presumably, that is why you're reading it.

But there *is* a further choice – one which will become increasingly promoted over the next few years, because there is a lot of money to be made from it. Newspaper readers recently opened their morning papers to read this amazing item: 'The ultimate wonder cure for a lousy lifestyle has arrived: the anti-cholesterol pill. Take one a day and you can go back to junk food, throw away the running shoes, and even take up smoking again and still escape a heart attack!'[4]

What could they mean? A stockbroker's analyst specializing in the pharmaceutical industry explained: 'The drug companies want people to ignore dieting, even though it is much more effective than drugs for 90 per cent of people. Ideally, the industry would like to prescribe anti-cholesterol drugs to everyone with a family history of heart disease – the market is enormous.'

'Which will be the next blockbusters?' asked the *Financial Times* recently, when surveying the extremely lucrative field of pharmaceutical products.[5] 'There is much speculation about the drugs now emerging from the research pipeline of the pharmaceutical industry which might turn out the big moneyspinners of the next few years.' The paper went on to cite two new cholesterol-lowering medications as being hot contenders. 'Each of these products, according to observers, has the potential of accounting for annual sales of hundreds of millions of dollars by the mid 1990s.'

Journalist and expert on the pharmaceutical industry, James Erlichman, also believes that anti-cholesterol drugs could be the next big money-spinners for the drugs business. 'You can usually tell when drug companies are revving up for a big sales drive,' he reports. 'They hold conferences in exotic places to foster scientific support for their products.' Recently, hundreds of doctors were invited to a symposium on atherosclerosis – held in Rome. 'The drug companies were throwing money about,' one doctor told Erlichman in confidence. 'It must have cost them £1,200 each for the 50 people they brought. We were put up in the finest hotels. Anti-cholesterols are the hottest property in the drug world and people are being hounded into their massive use even before some of the long-term trials are completed. In theory they allow people to live on hamburgers and sausages and yet have the blood cholesterol of a Chinese peasant who eats rice and soybeans.'[6]

In theory, then, they sound fine – providing, of course, you're happy to go on taking medication every day for the rest of your life. We asked Professor Michael Crawford what he thought about this new chapter in mass medication. He was not impressed.

'What this approach doesn't recognize is the underlying reason for the heart disease in the first place. If you just reduce the large amounts of cholesterol circulating in your body, you're just removing junk. It's rather like trying to remove water from the central-heating system when it's clogged up with scale – it's not an effective therapy in the long run, nor should it be considered as a solution to the problems which we can see starting to happen in young children.

'The evidence is very clear. Blood cholesterol starts rising in children from the age of seven. Between the ages of six and eight years, we can even begin to spot those children who come from high-risk communities simply by measuring the blood cholesterol and comparing them to children from lower-risk communities. That's got nothing to do with stress, or the amount of exercise they take, or smoking – fundamentally, this has really got to be a nutritional problem, which has to be tackled.

'Taking medication is not going to do anything for the health of the blood vessels. And it's the health of the blood vessels which determines both cardiac performance and – even more interestingly – brain function. Because the brain uses more oxygen per unit weight than any other tissue. And we know that when the blood supply to the brain is restricted, it doesn't do too well! A pill which reduces blood cholesterol will not avert the issue of cell growth in children, nor cell maintenance and repair in adults.'

Of course, a number of cholesterol-lowering drugs are already in use, mainly on patients who don't respond to any other method. We went to see a consultant who runs a clinic for such people, and asked him about drug therapy. He said:

'I don't give drug therapy without first trying to encourage the patients to make dietary changes. Only if that doesn't work, or if the patient is clearly suffering from familial hypercholesterolaemia, would I then use drugs. Of course, you must remember that drug therapy is for life. I find that many patients will try and make changes to their diet once they're taking drugs, because they want to stop taking them so much. I often have representatives from drug companies coming round to sell me something, telling me about the benefits of the latest drugs, but their trial data is often inadequate. And they don't always mention the side-effects. For example, a big practical objection to many drugs is belching – patients often produce a great deal of wind. But that's not always mentioned by the companies.'

It does rather seem, doesn't it, as if one person's cholesterol problem is another person's profit potential. Perhaps a few people *would* indeed be happy to put up with a lifetime of medication in exchange for the right to go on living and eating unhealthily. Of course, there is no guarantee that this Faustian bargain would be all it seemed to be – drugs sometimes have side-effects which only appear after several years of use. One drug – clofibrate, sometimes used to lower elevated serum triglycerides and cholesterol – is listed by the American Hospital Formulary Service as having an unpleasantly wide range of possible adverse effects, including nausea, vomiting, loose stools, diarrhoea, gastritis, flatulence, bloating, abdominal distress, cramps, weakness, decreased libido in men, impotence, and renal dysfunction. Little wonder that the AHFS warns: 'because there is no substantial evidence to date that clofibrate has a beneficial effect on cardiovascular mortality and because of the potentially serious adverse effects associated with use of the drug, clofibrate should only be used in carefully selected patients ... prior to institution of clofibrate therapy, a vigorous attempt should be made to control serum cholesterol and triglycerides by appropriate dietary regimens, weight reduction, exercise, and the treatment of any underlying disorder which might be the cause of the lipid abnormality.'

But Dr Bruce Kinosian, professor of medicine at the University of Maryland in Baltimore, has a further argument. 'If you can do it with diet, why use drugs?' he asks. 'There are clearly people who need drugs to lower their cholesterol, but there are other options out there that may be more cost-effective and are not being emphasized. There are a lot of people with high cholesterol levels in this country, and as a matter of social policy, you don't want to get in the habit of prescribing pills to everyone.' Dr Kinosian was one of the experts who undertook a cost-effectiveness analysis which compared using dietary means to lower blood cholesterol compared to cholesterol-lowering drugs. They found that an oat bran diet which is high in soluble fibre would be *just as effective* in preventing heart attacks as two commonly prescribed drugs – and of course, at a fraction of the cost. Dr Kinosian put the cost of oat bran at something like $40 a year.[7] One of the newest cholesterol-lowering drugs to come to market will cost about $3,000 a year. Quite a difference.

THE QUICK CHOLESTEROL CHECK-UP

Before you leave this chapter, you can quickly rate yourself against the following charts. Both are necessarily general, and do not replace the advice of your doctor. The first one concerns your existing cholesterol level which is measured in millimoles per litre, usually abbreviated to mmols. If you already know it, you can check the following chart to see how the advice of one panel of experts would affect you.[8]

5.2 mmols/litre or less

The desirable level. Do not make adverse changes to your lifestyle (smoking, fatty foods, lack of exercise, stress). Take another test in five years time.

5.2 to 6.2 mmols/litre

Borderline high. Follow cholesterol-reduction programme and take cholesterol tests annually. If you also smoke, have high blood pressure or are obese, cut out these risks. Some further testing may be necessary.

Over 6.2 mmols/litre

High. Follow cholesterol-reduction programme; cut out other risk factors. If no success, drug treatment may be necessary.

Although other bodies have set rather more liberal standards (the European Atherosclerosis Society, for example, suggests drug treatment for a persistent cholesterol level of 7.5 mmols or greater) the above targets make a reasonable framework to start from. Men between the ages of 40 and 59 can also answer the following questionnaire: [9]

Your Score

1. How many years have you smoked?
   Multiply this by 7.5 ....

2. What is your systolic* blood pressure?
   Multiply this by 4.5 ....

3. Has a doctor ever diagnosed angina or a heart attack?
   If yes, add 265 ....

4. Has a doctor ever diagnosed diabetes?
   If yes, add 150 ....

5. Do you have angina (chest pains while walking uphill or hurrying)?
   If yes, add 150 ....

6. Have your parents had heart trouble?
   If yes, add 50 ....

Total Score ....

SCORE	Risk of heart attack within 5 years
Over 1000	1 in 10
Over 890	1 in 30
Over 805	1 in 40
Over 690	1 in 100
Over 625	1 in 250

* Systolic blood pressure is the increased pressure which occurs with each beat of the heart, and is the higher of the two figures given when your blood pressure is taken.

Quick Summary

- Cholesterol is essential to your health, but when present in excess, can cause cardiovascular disease, heart attack and stroke.
- Two thirds of the population need to modify their diets to some degree to reduce their cholesterol levels.
- For every *one* per cent drop in blood cholesterol, there is a *two* per cent drop in the risk of cardiovascular disease – this is one game you can win!
- Our bodies require nutrients in certain proportions which our 'primitive' diet supplied, but which our modern diet does not – leaving many of us short of fibre, calcium, vitamin C and some essential fatty acids, but with too much total fat, saturated fat and sodium.
- You should always try to reduce your cholesterol level by natural dietary means before you consider using drugs.

2
THE LOW-DOWN ON HIGH CHOLESTEROL

We've just seen how cholesterol circulating in your blood-stream can slowly accumulate on the walls of your arteries, thus setting into motion a train of events which ultimately may prove personally catastrophic. At this point we need to do two things. Firstly, we must learn a little more about this sinister substance, so that we're better equipped to conquer it. And secondly, we must find out how, by using a variety of strategies, we can start to bring it under control again.

GETTING TO KNOW THE ENEMY

Picture yourself either sewing or using a sharp knife to perform a task which requires all your attention. Your mind wanders for a moment and – *ouch!* Clumsy. . . you've pricked your finger! Didn't your mother ever tell you not to play with sharp things? Not to worry, it isn't serious, but it *is* just enough to draw the smallest drop of blood to the surface of your skin. This droplet is, perhaps, no more than one cubic millimetre in volume. Yet, inside it there exists the most complex mixture of substances you could imagine. In round terms, there are roughly 5½ million red blood cells in that minuscule droplet, and each one contains haemoglobin, the oxygen-carrying protein which so efficiently transports its load from the lungs outwards to all the tissues. Each one of these red blood cells takes about a week to manufacture inside the red bone marrow that lies at the very centre of your ribs and vertebrae. During its short but hectic life, this little blood cell speeds around your body about once every 45 seconds. Fresh from the lungs, it takes on a bright red colour, which later changes to a bluish tinge after having delivered its oxygen to all parts of the body. After four hectic months, it will be consigned to the body's multi-purpose recycling plant located inside your liver and spleen, where it will be taken to bits and its component parts scavenged for useful knick-knacks.

In that same drop of blood, there also exist about 10,000 white cells. These are the crack troops in the body's front-line defence force against invading foreign bodies. Specific types of white cells have special defensive tasks assigned to them – some can engulf and devour invading bacteria (rather like a 'pac-man' gobbling up energy points in the old arcade game). Some of them can manufacture antibodies (which also have specific defensive jobs), and other white cells can target and destroy many other kinds of microscopic aggressors. Not the sort of blood cell you'd want to meet on a dark night – if you happened to be an invading bacterium.

Also present in that drop of blood are about 500,000 disc-shaped characters called platelets, whose task in the body's defence system is to close ranks and stick to any damaged area, thus helping the blood to clot and keep out unwelcome visitors. In fact, as you examine that little pin-prick closely, you will see those platelets happily start to perform their main task in life. The slight pain of the cut may have been unpleasant for *you*, but it really made those platelets' day!

All these tiny particles, and more besides, are kept in a state of movement and circulation because they are suspended in a watery substance called plasma. This is a rich chemical and biological soup, containing not only the cells mentioned above, but also various nutrients and hormones, as well as waste matter on its way to be junked.

As you examine this tiny drop of blood, which has already started to clot, you can actually see different parts of it begin to separate out. As the clotting agents begin their work, so they detach themselves from the medium in which they have been transported to the site of your minor injury. Look closely and you will see a pale yellow fluid around the wound. This liquid is called serum, and it consists of the remains of plasma after the clotting agents have gone to work. Now we're getting to the really important part, because this yellow liquid is of especial interest to us. Because, in addition to all its other transport functions, plasma also provides the medium in which cholesterol circulates inside us.

But it is here that the body faces a major problem. Cholesterol is a fat-like substance. Blood, on the other hand, is water-based. How, then, is the body to transport cholesterol in a watery fluid (without the result looking like a tacky French dressing – all oil on top, water underneath)?

The body's answer is characteristically ingenious. It does not try to mix fats directly with water, but instead, packages them into tiny parcels, which can then be washed around in the bloodstream with the rest of the fluids. At this point we need to use a few scientific labels, because there are several different types of packages, all with different functions and different names.

Your liver does most of this packaging work, and it does it by combining cholesterol with various substances (proteins) which *are* soluble in water. The medical name given to fat-like substances is 'lipid'. Therefore, when these fats, or lipids, are combined with proteins, the resulting substance is called a 'lipo-protein'. In a moment, we'll look at some of these lipoproteins in more detail.

First, let's mention something very similar to lipoproteins, but with a name that sounds as if it comes from a bad science fiction movie. Meet the chylomicron (pronounced ky-lo-my-kron). After you eat a fat-containing meal, vast numbers of chylomicrons surge into your bloodstream as your body begins to take apart the latest culinary offering, rather like a restaurant critic does. At first, a typical chylomicron only contains a small proportion of cholesterol, some of which will come from your food, and some of which is the original home-grown version. The main component, however, of a chylomicron is simply fat. To begin with, this little globule of fat mixed with a little cholesterol and a dash of protein circulates quite happily for a certain time, without being much disturbed by any bio-chemical process going on inside the liver. However, fat cells elsewhere in your body sense a free lunch approaching, and pretty soon most of the fat contained within the chylomicron has been scavenged, just leaving a saggy, cholesterol-rich particle referred to as a 'remnant'. It is now up to the liver to recover the cholesterol from this remnant, and thus remove some cholesterol from your serum. If it does its job effectively, your serum cholesterol level will not increase. But if your liver becomes slightly inefficient, the tendency will be for your serum cholesterol level to rise over time. Which is bad news.

Next on our suspect list are two real lipoproteins. The first is called 'pre-beta lipoprotein', or 'very low density lipoprotein', abbreviated to VLDL, and consists of 8 per cent protein, 20 per cent cholesterol, and a large amount of other fatty substances. The other is called 'beta lipoprotein' or 'low density lipoprotein', abbreviated to LDL, and consists of about 20 per cent protein and 45 per cent cholesterol. Most of the cholesterol you take in dietary form seems to make its first (but quite brief) appearance in your bloodstream in VLDL form. However, VLDL decays in the same way as chylomicrons do, and eventually their remnants become incorporated into LDLs – via an intermediate substance called, you'd never guess, 'intermediate-density lipoprotein'.

Now LDLs are the *main* carriers of cholesterol in your plasma. And as such, they are heavily under suspicion for complicity in elevating your cholesterol level. One of their functions seems to be to transport cholesterol away from the liver to other parts of the body. Now clearly, the liver (and other parts of the body, but mainly your liver) needs some method of keeping your LDL level under control, otherwise you would choke up with cholesterol sludge in a very short space of time. The way it does it is to have specific receptor sites located on cell membranes whose job it is to first bind the LDL particle to the cell, and then absorb it *into* the cell. These incredibly useful devices are called 'LDL receptors'. If you don't have enough of them, or if they aren't working very efficiently, your cholesterol level will climb.

At this point, out of consideration to our readers, we should ask 'how much more detail can you take?' If your head is already reeling, skip this paragraph. If not, let us mention what happens to the LDL particle once it has been absorbed into the receptor-containing cell. First, the protein is stripped away, generating free cholesterol. Well, not quite free, because the free cholesterol is quickly processed to a stable form and simply stored. At the same time, a chemical switch is thrown telling the cell that it now has enough cholesterol for its immediate needs, and it can stop producing it internally, thank you. This all sounds fine, but there is a problem. You see, biologically speaking, one of the functions of the LDL receptor (its *raison d'être,* in fact, if it's a French LDL receptor) is to obtain cholesterol supplies – if there's not enough in the bloodstream, then a message is sent ordering some to be made internally. But when cholesterol exists in abundance, as it does in many of us, there is less need for LDL receptors to thrive and flourish everywhere. Fewer are needed, because fewer receptors can grab as much cholesterol as they need from a rich supply floating by in the bloodstream. To put it simply, they get downright lazy! Consequently, an *excess* of serum cholesterol actually *decreases* the number of LDL receptor cells! Which is precisely what we *don't* need. Again, the end result may be the accumulation of more and more cholesterol in the blood.

Amongst all these highly suspicious particles, it comes as a relief to find one whose function is definitely benign. Let us introduce you to 'alpha lipoprotein', or 'high density lipoprotein' (HDL to its friends). This type of fat-protein complex consists of approximately 50 per cent protein and about 20 per cent cholesterol. Scientists believe that this substance is a 'good' lipoprotein, because one of its functions seems to be to scavenge for cholesterol in the arteries, on the artery walls, and from other tissues, and to transport it back again to the liver for safe disposal. Nice to have a few friends in there, isn't it?

So you can see, if you have proportionately more functional LDL than HDL, you could be in trouble. Because it's rather like having a six-lane motorway feeding a constant stream of traffic *into* a small town, yet only having one small country road to allow the congestion to *escape* from. Having too much LDL keeps cholesterol circulating in your blood – not having enough HDL stops it from being reclaimed and expelled.

Although there are good reasons for wanting the ratio between HDL and LDL to be as high as possible, there really is little convincing evidence that deliberately trying to raise your HDL levels, at the expense of ignoring other risk factors, will do much good. Although HDL certainly acts as a scavenger to remove cholesterol away from the arteries and back to the liver, there is, unfortunately, no satisfactory proof that simply raising HDL levels (which can be achieved in a number of ways, some of them healthier than others – for example jogging instead of drinking alcohol) will by itself lower your risk. On the other hand, there is a wealth of evidence to show that lowering your *total* cholesterol, and lowering the cholesterol carried in LDL form (and remember, about two-thirds of your body's cholesterol is carried like this) will *substantially* reduce your risk factors.

Now you know that cholesterol is transported around your body in a number of different forms. From this, it is easy to see that when you have a test for the amount of cholesterol in your blood (sometimes called serum cholesterol) it is also necessary to find out precisely *how* that cholesterol is being transported. Is it in 'good' HDL form or 'bad' LDL form? That's why, when you have a test, and the results show a higher than healthy level, your doctor will suggest that further tests be done to find out in *precisely* what form your cholesterol is circulating. At this point also, your doctor may well suggest another test for something called triglycerides. These fatty substances are, like cholesterol, both taken in with food and manufactured in the liver. They are used by the body to provide energy, and help us to store fat in our fat tissues. But triglycerides are not free from suspicion. As we eat more food containing triglycerides, it has been found that the rate of cholesterol absorption increases. Also, since they have an effect on blood clotting, someone with high triglyceride levels and with artery-narrowing atherosclerosis may suddenly suffer from a blocked artery due to a blood clot, resulting in a heart attack or stroke.

TRACKING DOWN THE KILLER

In the best of all possible worlds, none of us would have a cholesterol problem. The amount of cholesterol entering our system would precisely match the amount of cholesterol leaving it. There would be no atherosclerosis – no 'furred-up' arteries to slowly narrow and eventually reduce our blood flow to dangerous levels. In the best of all possible worlds, our bodies would do their jobs perfectly, and no-one would die from coronary heart disease.

Of course, we do not live in such a world. Heart disease is Britain and America's leading killer, accounting for the deaths of three out of every ten men and two out of every ten women. Every three minutes, it claims another victim. It is incredible, isn't it, that such an appalling and continuing human disaster – on such an enormous scale – could be caused by such a small amount of such an anonymous substance. After all, who's ever *seen* their own cholesterol? We have to take the scientists' word that it even *exists*!

Most of the cholesterol in our bodies is not a problem – in fact, it is a very necessary part of our bio-chemical nature, without which animal life would not exist. About 95 per cent of the cholesterol that your body contains performs its vital functions inside cells all round your body, helping them to maintain their structure and integrity. But it is the remaining 5 per cent or so which, while it is in transit in your bloodstream, seems to cause us such a problem. The truth of the matter is, this twentieth-century scourge of hearts seems to boil down to a question of balance. As Mr Micawber might have said, had he been around today: 'Cholesterol income 100 milligrams, cholesterol expenditure 100 milligrams, result happiness. Cholesterol income 100 milligrams, cholesterol expenditure 95 milligrams, result misery.'

The story of the painstaking detective work that lies behind the convincing relationship now established between dietary fat, cholesterol and atherosclerosis is itself a fascinating one, but sadly we don't have enough space here to cover more than one or two of the highlights. Most of the early evidence was gathered from extensive surveys of large numbers of people, and it is worth pausing for a moment to think about this pioneering work, because many thousands of people had to die to give us the knowledge we have today.

The first evidence linking our food to the development of heart disease came many years ago when scientists discovered that death rates from heart disease varied tremendously between one country and another. The first major study in this area compared the health of over 12,000 men who, at the beginning of the survey, were individually examined and declared to be free from coronary heart disease. After tracking the health of their subjects for many years, the researchers found that there was indeed a great disparity in deaths from heart disease between one country and another. In Finland, for example, thirteen times as many people contracted heart disease when compared to a similar group of Japanese people. Why should there be such a huge difference? Many more scientific studies were undertaken to try and find out. Despite the occasional red herring and blind alley, a very convincing pattern started to emerge.

One noteworthy study followed the health of 1,900 employees of the Western Electric Company over a period of twenty years. The purpose of the study was to see how diet, and particularly the type of fat it had contained, related to blood cholesterol, and also to find out whether a high level of cholesterol would result in more deaths from coronary heart disease. The study started in 1957, when all participants were thoroughly examined and questioned about their diet. When deaths had been tallied twenty years later, the researchers found that there was, indeed, a connection between a bad diet and deaths from heart disease.

The next question scientists wanted to answer was – if a high-fat, high-cholesterol diet increases your risk of coronary heart disease, can a low-fat, low-cholesterol diet *reduce* your risk? A number of researchers set about designing experiments to answer precisely this question. In Finland, two mental hospitals near Helsinki were chosen as ideal subjects, because the diets of the resident patients could be accurately measured and controlled. The basic experiment consisted of replacing dairy fats (which, of course, contain significant quantities of saturated fat and cholesterol) with vegetable oils (much lower in saturated fats). The design of the experiment is particularly interesting. Two hospitals were chosen because while one hospital tried the 'new' diet for a period of six years, the other hospital remained with the 'old' saturated fat diet. Then, after six years, the diets were changed over, and the hospital which had previously been eating a vegetable fat diet started to serve the old food again, and the other hospital started eating the new diet of vegetable oils and fats. And what was the result?

'The dietary changes,' said the researchers, 'were followed by marked changes in the serum cholesterol levels.' In the first hospital, the average patient's blood cholesterol level plunged by a staggering 19 per cent during the six-year period. When the second hospital adopted the vegetable fat diet, they too found that average cholesterol levels dropped by an impressive 12 per cent. In total, more than 4,000 patients were involved in the study. Perhaps most excitingly of all, the scientists found that during the period when the low cholesterol diet was being eaten, deaths from coronary heart disease dropped by 50 per cent!

More evidence that lowering blood cholesterol can reduce the risk of coronary heart disease came from studies conducted by the Lipid Research Clinics in America. In one study, about 4,000 men, all of them with a high cholesterol level, were divided into two groups. The first group, called the 'treatment' group, were given a drug (cholestyramine) to lower their cholesterol level. The second group, called the 'control' group were given a placebo (in other words, a completely harmless substance which would have no effect on their blood cholesterol). Neither the researchers nor the subjects knew whether they were taking the cholesterol-lowering drug or the placebo. After seven and a half years, the treatment group showed an average total cholesterol reduction of 14 per cent and – what is more – the treatment group managed to slash their risk of dying from coronary heart disease by 24 per cent.

It is impressive studies such as these, and many others like them, that have provided the evidence necessary for us to know that lowering our cholesterol levels is a very worthwhile thing to do.

CAN THE DAMAGE BE UNDONE?

Your body contains an impressive collection of systems, many of which continually restore and repair the damage you inflict on yourself simply by living. If your body can successfully repair the cut finger we so cunningly gave you at the beginning of this chapter, you may be wondering whether it can't also repair a rip in an artery?

Right now, the interest in many scientific circles has shifted towards answering precisely this question. Does the body have the capability to repair existing damage to an artery wall? If we lower a high cholesterol level, can we reverse the process of atherosclerosis? Can damage that has already been done to your arteries be *undone* just by lowering your blood cholesterol? The jury is still out on this one, but the signs are encouraging. There are already some interesting case histories where it seems to have happened, and some experts are beginning to admit that it may indeed be possible.

Apart from 'regression' (as scientists tend to call it), it is very encouraging to note, as well, that there *are* cases where the growth of atherosclerosis seems to have been halted in its tracks – even though existing damage to the arteries may not have been reversed. But the first case we could find concerning the regression of atherosclerosis occurred in 1977, when 25 patients (all suffering from high levels of blood lipids) were treated with a special diet and also with medication to lower their blood pressure. After just over a year, medical investigators found that thirteen patients had continued to develop atherosclerosis. However, three patients showed no change in the state of their disease, and – most excitingly – *nine patients showed 'significant regression'.*[10]

When researchers from the medical school at the University of California recently recruited 162 men to take part in an experiment to see whether the body can reverse the damage done to major blood vessels, they deliberately selected people who had previously undergone coronary bypass operations. Half of them ate a low-cholesterol diet and took cholesterol-reducing medication, while the remainder simply took a placebo. After two years, over 16 per cent of the test group showed 'significant regression' in the coronary arteries.[11]

Another study also seemed to show that about one-third of those patients who are given a low-cholesterol, low-fat diet, and who are also receiving drug therapy, *might* succeed in producing some regression of their atherosclerosis. At all events, many original sceptics are now prepared to admit that it *might* occur. The implication, of course, is tremendously exciting – it means that atherosclerosis is well worth fighting, with every weapon in your armoury.

HOW CHOLESTEROL OVERLOAD HAPPENS

As you've already begun to appreciate, cholesterol is a complex substance. Your body deals with it in a myriad of subtle and interconnected ways, and the processes we describe here are oversimplifications. Although we know *for certain* that cholesterol gradually builds up on artery walls, narrowing them until the odds are heavily against us, precisely *how, why,* and *when* are not quite so clear yet. But let's review a little more of the evidence.

It is remarkable to think that, in our society, few people can reach adulthood without having, deep within their bodies, the first but unmistakable signs of atherosclerosis – 'furred-up' arteries. From then onwards, most of us are simply playing for time – either hoping to put off further narrowing as long as possible, or maybe succumbing to another common illness before our arteries close in on us. Atherosclerosis is so common today that many of us perhaps consider it to be inescapable. But the truth is, in societies which lead different lifestyles and eat better diets than we do, coronary heart disease is almost entirely absent. In Kenya, for example, the first case of coronary heart disease was only diagnosed half-way through the twentieth century. Since then, however, Kenyan diets and lifestyles have become closer to our western 'ideal', and deaths from coronary heart disease have become a much more frequent diagnosis. This same pattern has been repeated in many, many other countries as they seek to emulate our western way of life – and death. It is, therefore, important for us to remember in all that follows that atherosclerosis, and coronary heart disease, is *not* inevitable. We can fight it.

One thing all investigators are agreed upon is that atherosclerosis consists of an accumulation of fats, primarily cholesterol, both on the surface wall of the arteries, and also inside 'foam' cells (cells which are swollen with cholesterol). Around this deposit proliferate an aggregation of smooth muscle cells, steadily growing, enlarging and blocking the artery. There are many theories as to how and why these crucial events take place, and the truth of the matter is probably that there are a number of major causes, acting together. For example, if some smooth muscle cells are penetrated by an external enemy – such as an invading virus or chemical – they may reproduce themselves very quickly, leading to a breach in the artery wall which then becomes an 'anchor' for cholesterol deposits and further cell growth. Another possibility is that blood platelets may stick together, deposit themselves on the lining of the artery, and so, again, produce a roughened surface on which cholesterol may accumulate. Yet another possibility is that high blood pressure may itself damage the lining of the artery, and again make it easier for lipids to be deposited there. There are probably a multitude of fundamental causes or precipitating factors.

So some form of damage to the lining of your arteries may be the first stage in producing atherosclerosis. But additionally, a high concentration of LDL in your blood may, *all by itself*, be responsible for damaging your artery walls. If the amount of LDL in your blood rises above a certain level, then it may manage to breach the artery wall. Normally, the cells lying on the wall, and just under its surface, will have their own ways of excreting cholesterol as it is produced or absorbed. However, if the concentration of LDL is so high as to prevent these cells from coping in the normal manner, then the cells themselves may be damaged, and turned into 'foam cells' which then go on to do so much damage to the lining of the artery itself.

The other crucial event in the development of atherosclerosis is the accumulation of a higher-than-healthy level of cholesterol in your bloodstream. But how does this 'cholesterol overload' happen? There is no one easy answer. We know that the liver plays a crucial role in cholesterol control. It is continually stripping cholesterol out of the bloodstream, and replacing it with newly packaged cholesterol which it then sends all over the body to perform its proper functions in cells. But just think – if you continually eat a high-fat diet, the liver will be *forced* to cope with this additional burden of fat processing, and one of the ways in which it will do this is to send the excess fat out into the fatty tissues of the body for storage (of course, this is one way in which people who consume fatty foods put on weight and become fat themselves). And as the liver assembles all this fat into little packages for transport, so it includes a little *cholesterol* in each one. The result? More and more little packages containing cholesterol circulating in your blood. And it will go on circulating until it's eventually reclaimed by your liver. But – here comes a serious problem.

One of your liver's duties is to make cholesterol if there's not enough to be found elsewhere (remember, we *need* some cholesterol). Now with so much cholesterol being taken in with your food (because a high-fat diet is usually a high-cholesterol diet), and with a fair bit of spare cholesterol already circulating in the bloodstream, there is absolutely no need for your liver to produce any home-grown cholesterol. There's masses already! So it cuts back on cholesterol production. Your liver now believes that there is more than enough cholesterol in the world for everyone, so it doesn't need to be so impressively efficient in reclaiming and recycling the cholesterol already circulating in your blood. Which is a big mistake, but at least you can understand how it happens. And the result of this decreasing efficiency of your liver will be a slow but sure build-up of cholesterol circulating in your bloodstream.

Now, if this theory is correct, then it might be possible to encourage the liver to become more efficient at cholesterol management simply by eating a diet which is lower in fats and extremely low in cholesterol. In this way, your liver would start to become more efficient in management of its own cholesterol, and become a good recycler of cholesterol in your bloodstream. The happy result of this would be a decrease in your blood cholesterol level, which is what we all want.

And here's another good reason to start eating a low-fat, low-cholesterol diet. People who are overweight have a lot of fatty tissue, which may *itself* be producing a significant amount of cholesterol. Normally, cholesterol effectively regulates its own production in cells, but it may not be able to do this in fatty tissue. Fat cells are precisely what they sound like – a huge greasy globule of fat sitting in the middle of a small cell, rather like Jabba out of 'Star Wars'. Very tasteless. There's not room inside for much else besides that fat globule, so any cholesterol which is produced is immediately dissolved in fat. Unfortunately, there simply may not be sufficient time for this freshly produced cholesterol to shut down the cell's cholesterol production mechanism – so the cell is deceived into thinking that it needs to produce *even more*. And this is how fatty tissue may be a significant source of serum cholesterol. Therefore, if you lose weight and reduce your fatty tissue, you may well *also* cut your cholesterol level into the bargain.

OTHER RISK FACTORS

These are just a few ways in which some scientists speculate that a low-fat, low-cholesterol diet works to cut back the level of cholesterol in your blood. Although the final answers may not be discovered for some time, there is absolutely no doubt that such a diet *can* be used to control cholesterol, and that it should be your first line of attack. But there's little point in taking dietary measures to reduce your cholesterol level if you're still going to lead a lifestyle that in other respects is essentially unhealthy. The fact is, you *do* have a number of different weapons in your armoury which will enable you to fight back against cholesterol, atherosclerosis and heart disease, so before we introduce you to the Quick Cholesterol Clean-Out diet, let's first examine some of the other main identifiable risk factors that are within your control and which, if managed properly, will fight the battle on your behalf.

Quick Summary
● LDL (Low Density Lipoprotein) are the main carriers of cholesterol in your plasma. HDL (High Density Lipoprotein) scavenges for cholesterol and transports it back to the liver for safe disposal.
● Having too much LDL keeps cholesterol circulating in your blood – not having enough HDL stops it from being reclaimed and expelled.
● Lowering your *total* cholesterol, and lowering the cholesterol carried in LDL form (about two-thirds of your body's cholesterol is carried like this) will *substantially* reduce your risk factors.
● Regression is possible! The damage that has already been done to your arteries may be undone simply by lowering your blood cholesterol.

3

GET READY FOR THE CHOLESTEROL CLEAN-OUT

Life is a gamble – every time you cross the road, you take a risk. Every would-be gambler knows that winning is just a matter of getting the odds stacked in your favour (which is why casinos win more than most punters). A casino, of course, stacks the odds pretty heavily against you, and there's not much you can do about it. But in the casino of life, the odds are much more flexible – and *you* can stack them in *your* favour! Each one of the following important factors can be controlled – by you – to reduce your risk of heart disease. We suggest you take action where appropriate.

HIGH BLOOD PRESSURE

Many people with high blood pressure don't know they have it until it is measured by their doctor. Others suffer from frequent headaches, chronic fatigue or kidney problems which eventually lead them to have a check-up. In fact, the general symptoms of high blood pressure can be quite vague. But there is nothing vague about the *effects* of high blood pressure on your heart and arteries. It is one of the leading causes of heart and circulatory disease and can result in handicap or death from heart attack or stroke. High blood pressure erodes your health, whether you are aware of it or not. It can gradually rise to an unhealthy level without you knowing a thing about it. This is why having your blood pressure measured once each year is a good idea.

Blood pressure is measured (usually by a doctor or nurse) using an inflatable bag which is wrapped round your arm. The inside of this bag is connected by a rubber tube to a mercury-filled pressure gauge. As the bag is inflated, the mercury rises within the pressure gauge, which is marked off in millimetres. When the bag is inflated to the same degree of pressure as that of the blood within your arteries, this flow of blood is briefly interrupted. By listening through a stethoscope it is possible to detect when this interruption occurs and to note the height of mercury within the gauge at this point: this is your *systolic* blood pressure, the first number in your reading. To obtain the *diastolic* blood pressure, the second number in your reading, it is necessary to listen to the pulse as the bag deflates and the mercury drops. Your diastolic pressure is recorded as the point on the mercury gauge when you can no longer hear the pulse. Now you have both figures – they are usually written like this:

BP = 120/80 mm Hg

It is, of course, normal and necessary for your blood pressure to vary according to circumstances, diet or even the time of day. But when your blood pressure is *always* high your health is probably in danger. This state is called hypertension and the person who suffers it is called hypertensive. The arteries and arterioles of a hypertensive person are more narrow and less flexible than in a healthy person. This means that the blood must push through them at greater force in order to circulate and the heart must pump much harder to maintain this circulation. Without sufficient pressure of blood in your arteries you would suffer dizziness, fainting or even death. Therefore, you need a blood pressure that is high enough to ensure proper circulation of the blood, but low enough to avoid damaging your heart and arteries.

Healthy arteries respond to changes in blood pressure by contracting or relaxing. Narrow, unhealthy arteries have lost their flexibility, so that blood circulating through them under high pressure can damage their inner linings. As you already know, when the lining of an artery is damaged, it is vulnerable to the build-up of cholesterol deposits. These deposits will further narrow and harden the artery so that the heart must work harder to circulate the blood through the system. The overall result is that your body *again* increases blood pressure to push all the blood through those restricted arteries. Which is how the vicious cycle of damage, narrowing, increased blood pressure and more damage is set into motion. Unless blood pressure is reduced as early as possible, this cycle of events may be repeated until something catastrophic occurs – such as a stroke or heart attack.

Unfortunately, hypertension often appears in company with other personal features or lifestyle habits that not only worsen this condition but can themselves increase your risk of suffering heart or circulatory disease.

SALT

Table salt or sea salt consist largely of sodium chloride. Sodium works with potassium in your body to balance the level of fluid inside and outside each cell. Too much of one or the other of these salts will create an imbalance. An imbalance – and it need only be a very small one – will create health problems particularly focussed on the arteries, heart and kidneys. High blood pressure is one of these problems.

Most of us probably take in more salt than is good for us so a general recommendation here to *reduce your salt intake* is in order. Here are three simple steps which can reduce your salt consumption by as much as half – without it being difficult or tiresome.

● Don't add salt to your food as you cook (except when cooking beans). Let each person add a little salt to their own meal when it arrives at the table, if they really want it. Taste tests have shown that food *tastes* saltier when the salt is added after cooking – even though less salt is generally used. And make sure that the salt shaker on the table is transparent and only one-quarter full. This seems to encourage people to use rather less than usual.

● Replace ordinary table salt with a balanced salt, such as Biosalt™, which contains potassium as well as sodium. Then add other condiments to your table, such as celery seed, dried herbs and spices, which will introduce other flavour-enhancing tastes – not necessarily salty ones.

● Shop with an eye for salty foods. Check the labels. Tinned foods, yeast extract and many 'instant' products are all potential salt traps – read the fine print carefully. Thankfully, many manufacturers have responded to consumer interest and produced excellent low-salt versions of many of these food products.

ALCOHOL

When it is part of a lifestyle 'package' that includes over-eating, smoking and lack of exercise, alcohol can contribute to liver and psychological disorders, obesity and, of course, heart and circulatory disease. The evidence implicating moderate alcohol consumption, by itself, in the development of cardiovascular disease is not strong, but there *are* strong indications that alcohol and other lifestyle habits – such as those just mentioned – together *do* cause cardiovascular disease.

It has been suggested that 'teetotallers' are actually at greater risk of cardiovascular disease than their alcohol-drinking friends. However, these benefits seem only to apply (if they exist) to very moderate, or low-level, drinkers who also keep their weight down and don't smoke. Other studies[12] point to alcohol consumption as a probable factor in the development of breast cancer. Certainly, most doctors agree that excessive drinking is not good for any aspect of your health. Obviously the choice is yours. But if you decide to drink you should know the risks and practice moderation – which is crucial if you wish to preserve your health.

So what are the risks?
- Alcohol can cause obesity and high blood pressure.
- Even moderate drinking during pregnancy can cause low birth weight and premature birth. Heavy drinking can cause deformity, blindness, retardation and heart problems.
- Alcohol taken with aspirin can cause abnormalities in the way your blood clots.
- Women may experience menstrual or gynaecological disorders from moderate to heavy drinking. Use of the contraceptive pill may, for some women, compound this effect.
- Men and women who smoke, over-eat or are overweight and who also drink will increase their risk of illness – of any sort – from this combination. Heart and circulatory disease is especially likely.

And what is moderate drinking?
- Women should consume *no more* than two to three units of alcohol, two to three times in a week.
- Men should consume *no more* than four to six units of alcohol, two to three times in a week.
- All drinkers should have three or four drink-free days in each week.
- All drinks should be consumed slowly: one unit per hour, one unit at a time, preferably accompanied by food.

One unit of alcohol equals:
    285 ml (½ pint) beer
    1 measure (a 'single') of any spirit
    1 glass wine
    1 small glass sherry
    1 glass vermouth or aperitif

A final caution – heavy drinking is *definitely* damaging to the heart, liver, stomach and brain. Avoid it!

OBESITY

Today, over 34 million Americans are so fat as to be considered 'obese' – that's one in every five adults. In Britain, the Government's COMA Report[13] revealed that there has been a progressive increase in the average weight of adults since the war until – currently – more than 40 per cent of middle-aged men and women are overweight. This figure does not include children. Currently, between 50 and 80 per cent of British children are thought to be overweight and underactive – these children are the obese adults of the future. Obesity is linked to the development of many serious illnesses, but in particular, high blood cholesterol levels occur *more than twice as often* in the overweight than in the non-overweight.

In fact, it seems likely that being overweight by only 10 per cent can greatly increase your risk of death from coronary heart disease, and this is especially likely in young men. Diabetes, hypertension and an increased level of blood cholesterol are all more likely to happen to you if you are overweight, and particularly if you have been overweight since childhood.

Many people learn to be obese as children and their bodies simply remain obese for the rest of their lives. This is hardly surprising when, as suggested by one health-care group,[14] nearly one-third of school children eat a lunch-time diet that is so high in fat it virtually *guarantees* they will suffer obesity and raised serum cholesterol levels later in life. Little wonder when, as the Department of Health's own survey (of the effects of abolishing school meals nutrition standards in 1980) has shown, four out of five children are eating an 'unhealthy' diet, including too much saturated fat and too few essential nutrients. They eat more chips, crisps, and other potato products than any other single food, and three times more chips, cakes, and biscuits than the average household.

Many voices have been raised in protest against the unhealthy diet that our children are eating, but not enough positive action seems to emerge. The 95,000-strong Assistant Masters and Mistresses Association produced a report which heavily criticised nutritional standards.[15] 'There is now ample evidence that our national eating habits are unhealthy,' it said, 'and it could be that education authorities, however accidentally, are reinforcing bad eating habits which children should be educated out of, not encouraged to carry over into the home.'

What is the answer to this epidemic of fatties? Ultimately, the root of the problem may lie with governments and food manufacturers, and it is perhaps only through developments in public policy that this crisis may be tackled. The fact is, most of us have a well-established diet and lifestyle by the time we're ten years old, and these patterns are often difficult or impossible to change in later life. If we've been taught bad eating habits, then we'll probably go on eating badly all our lives. And if we have been sedentary much of our childhood, we are likely to lead a sedentary lifestyle in adulthood, predisposing us to a wide range of physical and social problems. Sadly, today's children are underactive when compared with the children of earlier generations – especially so considering they have more calories to burn off. Their sedentary lifestyle is comprised of up to twenty hours spent watching television per week and greatly reduced numbers of hours spent in sports and games. Part of the blame for establishing an unhealthy diet and lifestyle early in life has to go to those parents who often say, 'We'll let our children decide what they want to eat for themselves, when they are older.' Do they think that *any* standards they present to their children are, in some way, impositions and mean deprivation? The real deprivation is this: the future of these children, their health and happiness, is in jeopardy because people who are overweight are more prone to depression, lack of confidence, guilt and frustration, and are often victims of a social prejudice that labels them as 'unattractive', 'greedy' or 'weak-willed'. They are also much more likely to suffer from cancer, hypertension and heart disease.

How have we got into this terrible predicament? Well, it seems we are simply taking too much of a "good" thing and not enough of what *will* do us good. Our food, the substance which *should* fill us with health and energy, seems to be turning us into diseased blobs who display little of the enthusiasm for activity that most other living creatures display. A diet high in fat is particularly to blame. The average person's intake of fat is approximately 40 per cent of their total calorie intake. Yet most medical recommendations[16] state that a *maximum* of 30 per cent is ideal. Set this against the fact that two-thirds of men and four-fifths of women don't exercise and, presto, there's big trouble in store. On the principle that what goes in must go somewhere, when we eat too much and exercise too little we SPREAD!!

The physical, mental and emotional consequences of obesity are clearly very serious indeed. And together they can act to immobilize you and prevent you from taking any corrective action. Yet that is precisely what you must do if you wish to break this vicious cycle. To reduce your weight you must commit yourself to making a gradual but permanent change in your diet and lifestyle. There really is no other way.

For most people, this means losing about 700-900g (1½-2lb) a week on a diet of about 1,500 calories a day for women and 2,000 calories a day for men. This is a gradual, but effective, approach to weight loss. 'Starvation' diets consisting of much lower calorie intakes may not be safe, and in any case, the most sensible approach to weight loss is to begin with a medical check-up to make certain that you have no special health problems.

You may estimate your degree of overweight by comparing your weight to that recommended for your height, gender and frame size (see the tables in the Glossary section). Generally, a 5 per cent excess implies that you are moderately overweight. Up to a 10 per cent excess means that you are overweight. Between 10 and 15 per cent excess is very overweight. Over 20 per cent excess weight above the ideal is considered obese.

If you are a young man who should weigh a maximum of 160 pounds (72.6kg), for instance, but you in fact weigh 176 pounds (80kg), then you are 10 per cent over your ideal weight (10 per cent of 160 is 16 pounds). This excess weight, however insignificant it may seem to you, *will increase your risk of coronary heart disease by approximately 30 per cent.*[17] This is because being overweight increases your likelihood of suffering high blood pressure and raised blood cholesterol levels. In fact, if you are overweight, you are between three and six times more likely to have high blood pressure and twice as likely to have raised blood cholesterol. Both of these disorders are directly responsible for many cases of cardiovascular disease.

The above example refers specifically to men, but don't think that being a woman offers you complete protection from cardiovascular disease. It is true that, for most women, risk of coronary heart disease is well below the risk to men for most of a woman's life. Her risk increases sharply after the age of 50, however, and, with that knowledge, many women may have relaxed into obesity. Don't! The incidence in women of death from coronary heart disease is rising – mostly due to an increase in women smokers, it's true. But it now seems almost certain[18] that women who carry excess weight, especially around their waist in what has been called a 'masculine' manner, run a higher risk of cardiovascular disease than slim women – no matter what their age.

Your risk can be reduced, however. Obviously if you smoke or drink large quantities of alcohol your risk from cardiovascular disease will decrease when you control these habits. Beyond that, it is imperative that you reduce your weight if you exceed the recommended limits by 5 per cent or more. Here is what we recommend:

● First, talk to your doctor and discuss the amount you have to lose. He or she may have advice or encouragement that you find particularly useful to your own circumstances. You can also put your mind at rest regarding any possible health concerns you have.

● Begin an exercise programme (see the section in this chapter) that will give you three or four 30-minute sessions each week. Choose exercise that you can succeed at and enjoy. Talk your ideas through with your GP, especially if you are very overweight.

● Begin a change of diet, such as the diet on which this book is based, which will reduce your intake of fat and excess calories.

● Eat at least three times per day so your body doesn't feel starved. Many people try to lose weight by fasting but, with a few food exceptions, *what* you eat is far more important to your health and eventual weight than *how much* you eat.

● Eat a high-carbohydrate diet so that 60-70 per cent of your food comes from whole grains, fruits, vegetables, beans, pulses and seeds. Prepare these without oils or salt.

Now stick with it! You already know that changing your shape and size can change your life. Why not go ahead and change your life – you will naturally change your shape and size as a result.

SMOKING

There is no doubt that smoking causes cardiovascular disease. In addition, smoking compounds the unhealthy effects of obesity, lack of exercise, high blood pressure and high levels of cholesterol so that, if you smoke, your total risk from cardiovascular disease is greatly increased.

Here is how smoking increases your risk:

● Smoking creates *twice* the risk of having a heart attack compared to non-smokers.

● Smoking *plus* high blood pressure *and* high blood cholesterol level creates *eight times* the risk of having a fatal heart attack compared to non-smokers.

● Heavy smoking (25 or more cigarettes per day) in men under the age of 45 creates *fifteen times* the risk of having a fatal heart attack compared to non-smokers.

● Women who smoke and take the contraceptive pill increase their risk of suffering ill-effects from this medication. Women who smoke and are over 35 years of age or overweight should stop smoking and consider changing their method of contraception. All women using the contraceptive pill should have their blood pressure checked regularly. (*Note:* The contraceptive pill is being continually altered in its strength and precise formulation and it is therefore likely that a change in the type of pill used will change the level of risk. It is also possible that new developments will completely or significantly reduce the risk associated with it. Discuss any queries you might have regarding the pill you take with your doctor.)

● Eight out of ten deaths from cardiovascular disease in young men are thought to be caused by smoking.

In chronic smokers the oxygen-carrying capacity of red blood cells can be reduced by 15 per cent. The reason is that cigarette smoke contains carbon monoxide which combines with the hae-moglobin in your red blood cells to form a compound called carboxy-haemoglobin. Carboxy-haemoglobin increases the permeability, or openness, of your artery walls so that more cholesterol is able to adhere to them. This is the beginnings of atherosclerosis and immediately increases your risk of heart attack.

If you are a smoker, your blood contains a poison that causes your arteries to narrow and your heart to work harder. In addition, nicotine, the addictive substance in tobacco, stimulates your nerves so that they constrict your blood vessels. This forces your heart to work *even harder* and faster in order to keep your blood circulating. Smoking creates ideal conditions in which to develop hypertension, atherosclerosis and, eventually, heart attack and death. That is without a mention of lung, throat and respiratory diseases – including cancer.

It really doesn't make sense to carry on smoking, does it? Especially when you realise that when you do stop smoking, your risk of suffering a fatal heart attack will begin to decline *immediately*. And within five to ten years you will have the same level of risk as a life-long non-smoker.

STRESS

Stress is a reaction to a situation, a person, an event. Anything can cause stress, anything can trigger a stressful response. Stress creates a sense of urgency which, though possibly arising from an emotional or mental reaction, nevertheless has physical symptoms too.

When you feel stressful, your adrenals make a hormone called adrenaline which prepares your body for immediate hard work and urgent action. This is a physical response – often called the 'fight or flight' response – which is an inheritance from our ancestors who used it to deal with dangerous situations. The situations in which we live are significantly different from theirs, but the same mechanisms are at work in our stressful responses.

During stress your body needs additional oxygen in order to help you either beat the problem or beat a fast retreat (fight or flight). To supply this oxygen, your heart beats faster and harder, your blood pressure rises and your rate of breathing increases. You also begin to perspire, anticipating the need to keep cool during your efforts!

To give you the instant energy you will need to fight or flee, your liver gets the stress message and triggers the release of fats and sugars directly into your bloodstream. This set of responses is an excellent means of ensuring self-preservation and will occur even when the stressful situation is left unresolved. In fact, much of our modern experience of stress is because we cannot resolve problems in the simple 'fight or flight' way. We have conditioned ourselves *not* to fight or flee, but to resolve our problems in a more 'civilized' manner. Unfortunately, our bodies haven't got the message yet.

Your body will react to stress in this age-old manner no matter how your social training tells you to respond. So, while you might *appear* cool, calm and collected, your body is still sweating and speeding – a case of 'all revved up and nowhere to go'. Other manifestations of stress are more apparent, and *very* common. They include asthma, eczema, headache, bad temper, indigestion and ulcers.

Unresolved stress can cause serious health problems and even death from stroke or heart attack. In the light of this possibility, it is imperative that each and every one of us learn to defuse stress before it takes its toll on us. One of the glossaries at the end of this book lists a number of contact organizations who specialize in stress management. We recommend at least one stress management technique in your life. Here are a few ideas to start with:

● Raise your stress threshold. Decide, and then train yourself, to become stressful only after all other possibilities have been considered. There really are dozens of options, apart from stress, including:

    laughing

    crying

    walking away from the problem

    making an appointment to solve the problem

    asking someone else to solve it

    asking someone to share it with you

    telling the perpetrator of it to go elsewhere

● Change the way you react to the stress in your life. If you currently internalize it, why not try hitting cushions instead! Or if you are a person who goes red with rage but still doesn't feel de-stressed, why not try some rhythmic breathing routines to expel the demon from your system. Here is the most basic breathing pattern for this purpose:

1. take one long, deep breath in
2. hold it for three seconds
3. then let the breath out slowly and, if you like, noisily
4. repeat this five to ten times – usually long enough to stop the stress reaction from developing fully.

● Take a nap! Researchers from the University of Athens, in Greece, studied people at risk from coronary heart disease and found that a half-hour nap in the afternoon could reduce their risk of heart attack by as much as 30 per cent. Elsewhere, scientists are 'discovering' what many people have known for ages – that holding and stroking a warm, furry animal soothes your *human* cares away too. In fact, it is possible that this gentle, sharing activity actually slows the heart beat and lowers blood pressure. What more encouragement do you need?

● Exercise combines movement, breathing, relaxation and the personal space and time for private contemplation. Just half an hour per day seems to dissolve worries, muscular tensions and those dreadful headaches that appear out of nowhere and are surely stress induced (see the exercise entry that follows).

EXERCISE

When the computer company IBM surveyed the health of its UK employees, it found that four-fifths of them were classified as 'unfit', and 32 per cent of them had a significant risk of heart disease due to high cholesterol levels in their blood.[19] 'They are not just a bunch of obese slobs,' said a medical officer. In fact, IBM's employees tend to live longer than the national average. 'It raises the question,' said the medical officer, 'of what the others are like if these are the results from a relatively healthy company.'

The survey found that 79 per cent of men and 75 per cent of women were obese according to standard medical definitions. On an overall measure, 83 per cent of men and 76 per cent of women aged 25 to 44 were found to be unfit. Only 6 per cent of men and 10.8 per cent of women were judged 'very fit'.

IBM paid for the cost of the health-screening programme (about £70 per employee), and is also investing a large sum in health-care facilities, including running tracks, gymnasiums and health-care experts. Now if a company such as IBM is prepared to invest considerable sums of money in its employees' health – presumably in order to keep them as productive as possible – shouldn't you also consider investing a little time and perhaps money in your own body? After all, an employee can always be replaced, but your body is the only one you're ever likely to be given.

If you can move and breathe and control your posture, then you can exercise, because exercise is only a particular way of combining movement and breath and posture. Virtually every moving activity you engage in can become an exercise if you add a special attention to detail and a special change in attitude. These special additions can be summarized as:

● an awareness of what is correct and appropriate exercise for you
● an eye for opportunities to improve your movement, posture and breathing patterns
● a willingness to learn and to achieve exercise skills
● an attitude of care towards your body

For example, walking your dog twice a day can be a chore which brings you slouching and grumbling out into the open air. Or it can be transformed into an opportunity to get a regular, brisk walk that will increase the strength of your heart and lungs, improve your stamina, muscle tone and possibly the health of your skin. It may also enable you to meet people or observe things you would otherwise have missed. Put like that, it sounds appealing, doesn't it? Yet the majority of us simply do not make the most of such opportunities.

An American study[20] found that 87 per cent of women and 68 per cent of men in their mid-forties do not exercise regularly. Here in the United Kingdom, a report[21] on the health of women showed that fewer than 20 per cent of women over the age of nineteen take regular exercise, even though most women know that regular exercise will benefit their health. This report was funded by the Association of the British Pharmaceutical Industry who no doubt want to know just how many of us will be in need of medication for cardiovascular ills in the near future. Quite a few, it seems.

That same American study[22] also found that men and women who are not physically fit have nearly three times the risk of dying from heart disease compared to those who are fit. The report states that 'a lower level of physical fitness is associated with a higher risk of death from coronary heart disease and cardiovascular disease'. Apparently, moderate exercise can reduce this risk. A 30-minute exercise session, three times per week, will get you fit and, in the words of Dr Basil Rifkind of the National Heart Lung and Blood Institute, which funded the study, 'fitness is protective against cardiovascular disease'.

How is fitness protective? The American study claims that both blood pressure and blood cholesterol levels drop in subjects who follow a fitness programme. In addition, this and many other studies show that regular exercise aids in weight control and stress management, both of which influence cardiovascular health. And exercise that challenges your heart and lungs, often called stamina or aerobic exercise, can literally strengthen the heart muscle and improve the efficiency with which you take in and circulate oxygen.

Regular exercise benefits the cardiovascular system by:
- reducing blood pressure
- reducing levels of cholesterol in the blood
- toning muscle tissue – including heart muscle
- increasing the efficiency of the heart at all times
- keeping the arteries flexible
- improving circulation and heart rate
- reducing stress
- reducing depression, aggression and hostility

These studies don't mention the other, more general, benefits of regular exercise which have been observed from ancient times. Most forms of exercise have the ability to reduce feelings of tension, both mental and muscular, and gently alter the mood so that you feel uplifted and alert a few minutes into your programme. And odd though it may seem, exercise can reduce fatigue. It seems that the energy you expend somehow returns to you in double quantity! Many people also claim an improvement in their balance, coordination and confidence after they have exercised for a few weeks. And, of course, many 'insignificant' aches and pains disappear once you begin to give your body the exercise it was designed to enjoy. Headaches, stiffness, sore joints and muscles, even cold toes and fingers can become ailments of the past.

Hopefully, we have convinced you of the hazards of not exercising, as well as the benefits coming if you do. The next step is to find an exercise programme that will suit you – your schedule, your environment, your age and interests. This is easier when you outline what you want in your programme.

For example, you may want:

● a group exercise such as a game or class *or* a solitary exercise
● a morning-only, daytime-only, evening-only, etc., exercise session
● an exercise that is silent *or* accompanied by rhythmic music
● exercise that involves a little expense, to keep you motivated
● exercise that is free except for the clothes you will wear
● a strict routine *or* a lot of variety
● three or four seasonal exercises *or* one year-round exercise

Do you get the idea? There are many more options that could be added to this list, but we're sure you will discover your own preferences once you give it a bit of thought. We must stress, however, that exercise is most effective when it is an integral part of your life, so that you feel something important is missing when you do *not* exercise. For this reason alone, it is best that the exercise programme you select is pleasurable.

Many people start to exercise regularly but then something happens which gets them out of the routine. In fact, this has probably happened to even the most committed athletes, at some time or other. The difference is, the committed people start up again, but the rest of us say something like 'I just can't find the time any longer.' We found our reply in an old quip which states: 'If you don't have time for exercise, you'll certainly have time for illness.'

We urge you to pick two or three types of exercise and practise them on a rota basis, to accommodate sudden changes in your schedule or circumstances. For instance, if you take up jogging but can't stand jogging in the rain, you could use a skipping rope in your front room on the mornings that it rains. Similarly, you can cycle indoors all the winter, walk spring and autumn and swim in the summer. And if the babysitter doesn't turn up on the day you are scheduled to go swimming, you can spend 20 minutes on the rowing machine or take to that skipping rope again.

Here is a summary of essential considerations when planning or beginning an exercise programme:

Pick exercises that cause:
the muscles to both stretch and contract
the joints to move
the brain to deal with coordination
the lungs to open for deep breathing
● the heart to pump strongly and regularly

Exercise a minimum of:
● three times each week
30 minutes per session

Each 30-minute session includes:
● warm-up movements
the exercise of your choice
● cool-down movements

Exercise to the point where:
● you become *slightly* breathless, but are always able to speak clearly

Do NOT exercise if:
● you are ill
● you are injured
● you are undernourished
● you are *very* tired, physically, mentally or emotionally
● you have already exercised today
● you have a medical condition which requires a doctor's advice –
get his or her opinion on the exercise programme you wish to follow

Here are a selection of activities that can provide effective exercise for your heart and lungs. Please follow the guidelines just listed when performing any of these exercises. The summary for each exercise follows the format:
● where or how is it done?
● how long is it done for?
● why or for whom is it especially beneficial?
what are its special attractions?
what are the clothing requirements?

what are the drawbacks or disadvantages?

Cycling

indoors on a stationary bicycle *or* outdoors on a geared bicycle
minimum of 20 minutes without stopping
especially good for the elderly or those with hip or back problems
● little likelihood of injury to muscle, tendon, ligament, etc.
wear non-chafe clothing and a helmet for outdoor cycling
outdoor cyclists should plan a safe, non-stop route with few hills

Dancing

ballroom, rock 'n roll, disco, folk, Scottish country or any other
minimum of 12 minutes without a complete break
● very social and pleasant for those who like music and rhythm
an attractive activity which makes one feel competent and co-ordinated
● wear flat, comfortable shoes to avoid foot injury
● dance with a partner who can also dance for 12 minutes!

Games

● volleyball, squash, tennis, golf or similar
● minimum of 30 minutes as these are usually stop-start activities
● especially good for those who like to compete or follow a set of rules
social yet with a chance for individual accomplishment and skill
● wear shoes and clothing suited to the game, allowing free movement
● play with a partner who will challenge you, but not too much

'Jarming'

● sitting in a chair and 'jogging' with your arms
● minimum of 15 minutes without stopping
● particularly for those who are elderly or in any way infirm
● achieves cardio-respiratory goals safely and effectively
● may be performed to rhythmic music
● maintain a size and pace of 'jarm' that will allow adequate breath

Jogging

● in an indoor court *or* outdoors on track or field
● minimum of 15 minutes without stopping
● for those who are able to exercise strenuously without pain
● may be social or solitary with scope for competition if desired
● select very supportive shoes and non-chafe clothing
● weather, dogs and mud are always hazards

Keep-Fit

● in a class *or* at home using an audio cassette or video tape
● minimum of 30 minutes

for a complete fitness programme of stretch, strength and mobility
for all ages; classes are usually very social and full of variety
wear loose or stretchy clothing
- make sure your teacher is qualified and gives you personal attention

Rowing

on an indoor machine *or* join an outdoor rowing club!
minimum of 15 minutes without stopping
- an excellent way to exercise the whole body
- for all ages; having particular effect on arms, legs, back and abdomen
- wear minimum, non-chafe clothing
- indoors, select a machine with a sliding seat

Ski-ing or Skating

- cross-country ski-ing or ice or roller skating
minimum of 20 minutes without stopping
- all the benefits of running or jogging
- mostly lower-body exercise, though arm movement improves breathing
- wear stretchy, non-chafe clothing and appropriate skis or skates
ski-ing is seasonal, and you need to find rink space for skating

Swimming

- in the United Kingdom, usually an indoor exercise
- minimum of 20 minutes without stopping
- excellent to loosen joints and muscles and improve heart and lungs
- a variety of strokes ensure the majority of joints and muscles are used
- wear minimum clothing
- finding a clean, uncrowded pool is sometimes difficult

Walking

- an anywhere, any-time activity
- minimum of 20 minutes without stopping
- an excellent exercise for heart, lungs, back and lower body
- for all ages; a no-trauma way to travel, entertain yourself or exercise
- wear high-quality supportive shoes
- it is necessary to maintain a brisk pace for maximum benefit

Weight Training

- using a multi-gym or poly-gym arrangement in a sports centre
- aim for 20-30 minutes of sustained training
improves strength, muscle tone and posture in specific body areas
- for all ages; provides an opportunity to become more physically aware
wear supportive shoes and loose or stretchy clothing
a qualified coach is essential in your first month of training

Yoga

- at home from memory *or* at a class run by a certified teacher
- most classes last at least 1 hour, some up to 2½ hours
- increases your mobility, suppleness, posture and improves breathing
- for all ages; also gives you time and mental space to contemplate
- wear loose or stretchy clothing and have an extra layer at hand
- it can take time to find the teacher and type of yoga class that suit you

PSYCHOLOGICAL ADJUSTMENT

Any change in your lifestyle, even one that you invite, is bound to require a degree of effort on your part. In all of the aspects of lifestyle just discussed, most of the emphasis was placed on physical changes – on how this or that will affect your body – and physical effort. Certainly much of what we discuss and recommend in this book has physical consequences, but we feel it is important to mention the psychological – the mental and emotional – effort and changes that can also occur.

It is a fact that when you change your diet, your sleeping habits, your level of fitness or any of the other influences mentioned, you automatically alter your inner self too. When your body feels better, for instance, your outlook improves. And the reverse is also true: when you improve your outlook, you usually feel better physically. It seems sensible then, to use this link between your body and your inner self to help make the change to a healthy lifestyle more effective and more pleasurable.

We have devised a simple check-list which will help you recognize the role your inner self can assume during your change to a state of low-cholesterol good health.

- *Learn the facts*

Give your brain some work to do while your body is making changes to diet, drinking and exercise habits. Read and listen to what you can about each subject so that you become familiar with the terminology and the most current research.

- *Learn to listen*

Each physical change affects you mentally and emotionally, if you just listen to your feelings. Sometimes long-standing issues are resolved by dropping alcohol, cigarettes or obesity from your life. When you have felt this happen once, you are more likely to believe it can happen again.

- *Learn to choose*

Sometimes you need to make one change at a time in order to change successfully. There is nothing wrong in this. In fact, many people find the change is more likely to be permanent if it is done one step at a time. It is up to you to choose which step to take first. . . and second. . . and third. . .

● *Learn to plan*

When you at last spring into action, it is important to have a plan. Your inner self is especially good at these. Write down the action you will be taking, when you will start and what your goals are. Then pin it to your wall and go!

● *Learn to forgive*

When you make a mistake, lose your way or just plain turn your back on the whole thing you commit a very human act. But don't let yourself fail just because of that! Forgive yourself and then start up again, now!

● *Learn to reward*

When you achieve a goal, however small, treat yourself to praise and a present. You deserve it.

● *Learn to take charge*

The decisions and junctures in your life are yours to determine for yourself. Take possession of and responsibility for your life, your body, your thoughts and feelings. Accept your life as your own and enjoy even those elements of life over which you have no control. Taking charge leaves you in a position to *create* change and opportunity and to determine the course your life will take.

GET CHECKED!

Before we outline the very practical dietary steps which you may take to reduce your risk of cardiovascular disease, you should arrange to have your cholesterol level and your blood pressure checked by your doctor. If you have a family history of heart or vascular disease, if you smoke or are obviously overweight then you become a member of the 'high risk group' as far as cardiovascular disease is concerned. Your risk of suffering heart attack, for instance, is considered greater than in someone who does not display these obvious signs of risk.

However, many people do not visit their doctor very often or may not feel that they fall into these high-risk categories. Nevertheless, they may be at great risk! Both blood pressure and cholesterol are renowned for rising gradually and 'silently' to dangerously high levels – without you knowing anything about it until something drastic happens.

The fact is that most of us in this country are at great risk from cardiovascular disease. Approximately 60 per cent of us have cholesterol levels which place us in the high risk category.[23] We know *why* so many of us fall into the high risk category, but we have done little about it – perhaps because poor diet, obesity, smoking and general ill-health has become 'normal' to us. What a state!

So, ring your doctor's surgery (today!) and make an appointment. Tell the receptionist that you want to have your cholesterol level measured and your blood pressure checked. It's that easy. No-one will ask you embarrassing questions over the 'phone. Then just turn up and roll up (your sleeve!).

TESTING YOUR CHOLESTEROL LEVEL

The test for blood cholesterol level requires a sample of your blood and this is usually taken from your arm. Strictly speaking, you do not have to fast before you have this test. However, many doctors feel that your triglycerides might as well be measured at the same time and, for this test, you do have to fast for a period of approximately sixteen hours. This usually means that you don't eat anything after 8 o'clock the evening before your appointment and nothing during the morning on the day of your appointment.

You should ask the receptionist, when you make the appointment, whether the doctor will want you to fast or not. This is important. Fasting isn't fun for everyone and it would be frustrating to arrive at the surgery with audible hungry pangs only to be told you needn't have fasted.

One other point, some doctors will not take the blood sample themselves but will give you a slip of paper and send you to the local hospital to have your test there. The receptionist might know if your doctor prefers this method.

A growing number of health centres in this country are acquiring a machine which is able to give a fairly immediate cholesterol level measurement just by taking a finger-prick blood sample. If you attend one of these centres, you can get your results within a few minutes of shedding that drop of blood. On the other hand, if you have a standard blood sample taken from your arm you could have to wait up to a fortnight before the results come through to your doctor. This means that you will need to make another appointment to learn the results. And you *must* learn the results!

When you attend your second appointment, ask your doctor to write down your blood cholesterol level on a slip of paper for you. If your triglycerides were measured, ask for that result to be noted down as well. It is very important that you know these figures. When your doctor sees your interest, he or she may offer you advice on diet or lifestyle. Take this opportunity to discuss the implications of your cholesterol level and to inform your doctor that you intend to try reducing your blood cholesterol level through diet, if you haven't informed them already.

Quick Summary

Your risk from cardiovascular disease can be greatly reduced by following this five-point lifestyle plan:

1. Stop smoking
2. Control your weight and level of stress
3. Reduce your salt and alcohol intake
4. Take regular exercise
5. Alter your diet

We've talked about the first four. . . . Now all that remains is for you to start reducing your risk of cardiovascular disease by following the Quick Cholesterol Clean-Out diet. So turn over the page, and turn over a new leaf!

4
THE QUICK CHOLESTEROL CLEAN-OUT

Are you ready? Good! For the next six weeks or so, the food you eat will be working *for* you to reduce the amount of cholesterol circulating in your blood. Our research has shown that certain foods have the ability to remove cholesterol from your blood, so we have designed a range of quick, easy and satisfying meals that include these wonderful 'cleansers'. You might be surprised to learn that many of these foods are basic, much-loved staples which you probably have in your cupboard right now!

One of the keys to cholesterol reduction through diet lies in eating foods which are high in a certain type of soluble fibre. Such foods have a viscous, gluey or glutinous consistency when they are cooked, indicating the presence of this particular type of fibre. Most of us are familiar with the term 'fibre', but probably only with the idea of *insoluble* fibre, sometimes called 'roughage', which is not digested in the gut. Instead, it helps in the passage of waste material through your digestive system and contributes to your good health in many other ways. *Soluble* fibre, however, is a rather new idea to most people, and for those who want to learn more about it, we've included some more information in Chapter Six. However, the most important thing you should know about soluble fibre is that certain forms of it *have the ability to remove cholesterol from your blood*.

Natural foods high in this type of soluble fibre include **oat bran** and **beans** – others are mentioned in Chapter Six. They produce that gluey substance when they are cooked, which indicates their suitability for the job we have in mind. We have included a significant amount of both foods in the meals that follow because a large serving of these foods, eaten on a daily basis, can cause a reduction in your cholesterol level! This effect is referred to in scientific literature as a 'hypocholesterolaemic' effect, and there is abundant evidence (some of it mentioned in Chapter Six) to prove that these foods *really do work*. These foods provide the framework for the Quick Cholesterol Clean-Out because they can start to reduce your cholesterol level without the help of drugs.

However, we don't stop there. The Quick Cholesterol Clean-Out is also low in fat. For six weeks you will be eating a very low-fat diet that is also completely free of dietary cholesterol. In other words, the foods you eat won't have any cholesterol in them and very little fat. Why? To answer, let's look briefly at how fat and cholesterol affect each other.

CHOLESTEROL AND FAT

Cholesterol is a fatty substance that is already present in your body. It is also present in the bodies of other creatures so when you eat foods of animal origin you take in extra cholesterol. This cholesterol (called dietary cholesterol because you had to eat it to get it) has to be processed by your body and some of it will be absorbed into your system. Precisely how much is absorbed depends on a number of variables, but is closely related to the amount of *fat* you consume.

You need a certain amount of fat in your body just to keep well (it carries nutrients like Vitamins A, D and E, for instance), but most of us eat a diet which is much too high in fat – perhaps taking in twice as much as we really ought to. When you eat a diet high in fat, you create an opportunity for more cholesterol to enter your bloodstream. When you eat a diet high in *both* fat and cholesterol, you create a 'timebomb' situation where your body is accumulating more and more fat, and circulating more and more cholesterol. At a certain point your body may be unable to remove surplus cholesterol from your blood at the same rate that surplus cholesterol is being added to your blood. Things get badly out of balance, and this is the point at which cholesterol begins to deposit on your artery walls, causing the disease process called atherosclerosis. The higher the level of cholesterol in your blood, the more rapidly it will be deposited on your artery walls.

So, in the Quick Cholesterol Clean-Out we have reduced your intake of total dietary fat to 20 per cent of your total calorie intake. This is *half* of what is considered to be the current average daily intake of fats. By itself, a reduction in total dietary fat is known to be beneficial to health – at least in countries where people are generally very well fed – and this step alone would probably result in a considerable reduction in this country's rate of death from heart disease.

Some of the dietary fat you obtain during the six-week period comes from the olive oil you add to your Special Oat Biscuits (the reason we're keen on olive oil is explained in Chapter Six). The remainder is naturally present in the foods you eat. Oats, beans, vegetables, fruits and grains all contain small quantities of fat which are either polyunsaturated, saturated or mono-unsaturated. Their presence in these foods is useful when your body tries to assimilate the fat-soluble vitamins, for instance. Of course, we have avoided adding very fatty natural foods, such as avocados, to the diet in order to maintain the 20 per cent goal we have set. Most importantly, because you won't be eating any animal-based foods during the diet period, you greatly reduce your intake of *saturated* fats. These, of all the fats, are thought to be most responsible for the elevation of blood cholesterol levels.

NUTRIENTS

Although we have taken the very fatty and animal-based foods from your diet, we have included foods that are rich in vitamins and minerals. In fact, we think you may be better nourished on this diet than on a conventional diet with double the percentage of fats! You might find, however, that for a time you miss the 'heaviness' of your previous, high-fat diet. This is not surprising, considering that fat takes much longer to digest than complex carbohydrates. A high-fat meal simply hangs around in your gut for longer, making you feel 'satisfied' (or feel indigestion!) for longer too.

We ask that you have patience while your body gets used to the transition from high-fat food to high-nutrient food. Your body will make the transition quite quickly if you give it the chance, and it will benefit from the transition as well. And not just because the food in this diet is packed with vitamins and minerals: the food you will be eating during this six-week period is high in complex carbohydrates. Foods high in complex carbohydrates are also the only foods which can be rich in fibre, both soluble and insoluble, which has a very special role to play in reducing your level of cholesterol and therefore your risk of suffering coronary heart disease.

CALORIES

No matter how you choose your day's diet, we've arranged each menu so that it comes to approximately 2200 calories – which is the average requirement for a woman aged 18 to 54 (women over 55 need slightly less). It is also adequate for many men who are obese, and therefore in need of a reduced-calorie diet. However, if you find you need more food, please give yourself bigger portions by extending the recipes by one-quarter or one-half; or you can follow the additional recipes listed later in this chapter. If you find you need fewer calories, then reduce the size of your portions a little, but don't skip the biscuits! You will find that we strongly suggest a good breakfast in the morning, so please don't be tempted to skip it, or just 'make do' with a slice of toast and a glass of juice.

MEAT'S NOT NEAT . . .

The Quick Cholesterol Clean-Out doesn't include meat in the diet for obvious reasons – meat, being a prime source of both cholesterol and saturated fats, is about as useful on a low-cholesterol diet as a bottle of vodka is to a reformed alcoholic! And we're pleased to say that, when put to the test, none of our valiant band of subjects who tried the menus in this book reported that they missed meat products at all during the six-week period. However, if you feel you want to eat meat or fish products after this six-week period then *The Quick Cholesterol and Fat Counter*[24] will help you to find the less-fatty, lower-cholesterol types. But before that, we have a suggestion for you to consider. Try some of the excellent 'new meat' type products which are becoming available now. Brands such as Tivall, Worthington, Realeat, Granose and Protoveg can all be found in health food shops and many supermarkets, and are identical to meat in their flavour and texture. However, they are *different* to butcher's meat because they *don't* contain the fats and cholesterol which makes meat products such a killer. So give them a try! When you consider that an animal-fat-free diet slashes your risk of developing coronary heart disease by 57 per cent,[25] there really aren't any good reasons not to try it.[26]

Now we come to fish. In recent years, eating fish, and particularly consuming fish oil, has been widely promoted as an effective way to reduce the risk of coronary heart disease. Although there is some evidence that some fish oil consumption may indeed reduce mortality from coronary heart disease, we would caution you against the indiscriminate use of *any* drug or supplement unless you are under medical supervision. Fish oil is rich in omega-3 fatty acids, and in particular in eicosapentaenoic and docosahexaenoic acids, which are believed to be able to lower triglyceride levels. But can fish oil reduce your cholesterol level? 'There's no proof fish oil lowers the LDL cholesterol level', said Dr John C. LaRosa, of the George Washington University Medical School and chairman of the First National Cholesterol Conference in Arlington, Va. 'If it does help prevent heart disease, it's probably by affecting the way blood clots form.'

In fact, the case for fish oil is by no means conclusive. In one scientific trial, it was found that although fish oil supplements caused a decrease in serum triglycerides, they also caused a fall in 'good' HDL -cholesterol and a rise in 'bad' LDL -cholesterol. The researchers concluded that 'the small adverse effects on cholesterol might negate any beneficial effect on the atherosclerotic process'.[27]

Another study investigated the effects of a fish oil supplement on 31 patients with high blood cholesterol levels, and found that although triglyceride levels fell, *all* cholesterol levels rose significantly – total cholesterol soaring by 14 per cent in just 28 days. 'These results suggest' wrote the scientists, 'that fish oil supplements may have an adverse effect on lipid/lipoprotein values in hypercholesterolemic patients.'[28]

'The fish oils that are promoted as providing protection to the arteries', states Dr Michael Klaper, an internationally-known health educator, 'may also pose a serious hazard because they decrease the body's ability to coagulate blood to stop bleeding. Eskimos, who eat large amounts of fish, suffer high rates of haemorrhagic strokes, nose bleeds and epilepsy.'

Vegetarians and others who do not wish to consume fish should note that omega-3 fatty acids can also be obtained from non-animal sources – flax oil, for example, is a rich source, and is both cheaper and of greater strength than fish oil. Walnuts, walnut oil, wheat germ oil, soya lecithin and seaweed also contain lesser sources of omega-3s (fish themselves obtain it by eating plankton and other sea plants).

But since they affect a wide range of biological processes, omega-3 fatty acids should be used carefully. One study shows, for example, that omega-3 fatty acids can have a 'significant deleterious effect' on people with non-insulin-dependent diabetes.[29] Other problems linked to the consumption of fish oils include their suspected involvement in gallbladder disease, and the possibility that they may promote cancer. 'An unpublicised, but potentially important problem' says Dr Michael Klaper, 'results from fish oil's apparent tendency to increase the length of a normal pregnancy. An overly long gestation time increases the birthweight of the baby, and thus the attendant risk of birth accidents. Despite current advertising campaigns, no one needs to eat the oil squeezed out of a fish's flesh or liver; in fact, the products of a fish's liver is one of the strangest substances to consider eating. The liver of any animal is the chemical detoxifier for the body, and thus concentrates all the pollutants consumed by that animal. The oil squeezed from fish livers can contain high levels of toxins (such as PCBs, DDT, dioxin and heavy metals) plus large amounts of cholesterol.'

One thing is for sure – omega-3 oils are no panacea, no 'magic pills' that will miraculously allow you to continue eating a bad diet without clogging up your arteries. Attending to the root cause of our health problems is the only sure way to a cure.

WHAT ABOUT THAT CUPPA?

If you are a tea or coffee drinker, please make a special effort to stop at least during the course of this diet, because there is evidence that caffeine can raise your blood cholesterol level. In any case, there are many alternatives – herbal teas, mineral waters, cereal coffees etc. Again, most supermarkets have a wide range of these products available so please experiment until you find something which suits you. Also, please make a special effort to avoid dairy milk and use soya milk instead. The Plamil® company produces several varieties of soya milk, all of which are available at health-food shops and some supermarkets. We think the Plamil® range is, nutritionally, the best type available and well worth the extra effort you might expend to find a local source. You will probably benefit from increasing your intake of fluids during this six-week period but, if you are going to drink alcohol, please restrict your intake of alcohol to a maximum of 2 units per day, and preferably less. See page 38 for alcohol unit chart.

CLEAN-OUT!

We are suggesting that it's time you gave your arteries a holiday! By temporarily halting your intake of dietary cholesterol, it seems possible that the cholesterol already in your system will be circulated to your liver, which may then remove it from your system in the same way it does other waste material. By greatly reducing your dietary fat during this same period, you will further stimulate your body to dispose of excess cholesterol in the blood.

We hope you enjoy this diet and, more importantly, that you find it effective in reducing your cholesterol level and bringing about a greater sense of well-being. And just to show you that the Quick Cholesterol Clean-Out doesn't have to be all fast food, we have included ten whole days of Quick Cholesterol Gourmet menus in the next chapter. Dieting was never like this! Now you're ready to start . . . but first remember to:

● get your cholesterol level checked by your doctor and get your doctor's approval to start the diet.
● learn the results and make another appointment for six weeks' time.
● begin the diet – either the Quick version or the Gourmet version.
● return for your second cholesterol level test at the end of six weeks.
● keep your cholesterol level low using the Cholesterol Control diet.

THE QUICK CHOLESTEROL CLEAN-OUT DIET

Every Day . . .
● Eat twelve Special Oat Biscuits each day *without fail*.
● Eat three meals per day, choosing one meal from each of the Breakfast, Lunch and Dinner selections that follow.

Breakfast
Choose one from this selection each day for six weeks:
● Fruity All Bran® cereal with Apple Juice and Fresh Banana
● Apple Porridge with Apple Juice and Fresh Banana
● Easy Muesli with Grapefruit Juice
● Speedy Fruit Bowl with Crisp Toast
● Toast and Marmite with Apple Juice, Fresh Banana and Orange
● Bubble 'n Squeak with Beans on Toast, Grilled Tomatoes and Grapefruit Juice
● Split Banana filled with Berries and 'Cream' with Crisp Toast and Grapefruit Juice

Lunch
Choose one from this selection each day for six weeks:
● Baked Potato filled with Baked Beans or Sweetcorn and Chopped Tomato with Apple Juice
● Lentil Soup with Crackers and Marmite, Fresh Banana and Grapefruit Juice
● Baked Beans on Toast and Fresh Apple
● Mixed Salad Platter: Bean Salad, Green Salad and Pasta Salad
● Hummus Sandwich or Pitta with Green Salad, Fresh Orange and Apple Juice
● Rice Salad with Apple Juice
● Two Salad Sandwiches with Fresh Banana and Apple

Dinner
Choose one from this selection each day for six weeks:
● A starter of Grapefruit Segments followed by Spaghetti with Hi-Protein Tomato Sauce
● A starter of Melon followed by Bean and Cauliflower Curry over Rice
● A starter of Green Salad followed by Easy Vegetable Casserole
● A starter of Grapefruit followed by Stuffed Peppers on a bed of Rice
● A starter of Tomato Soup followed by Mushroom and Lentil Pie
● A starter of Raw Vegetable Crudités followed by Macaroni Bean Bake
● A starter of Fresh Berries followed by Sweet 'n Sour 'Pork' over Rice

The following recipes are written for one person. If you wish to prepare them for your partner or another member of your family, simply double the quantities given. (However, the portions are already quite large so you may find yourself sharing in any case.) These meals are based on popular dishes so even if your spouse is *not* trying to lower their cholesterol level, they can still enjoy them! Alternatively, you may prefer to try the Low-Cholesterol Gourmet in the next chapter to enjoy ten ready-made menus which have already been specially created for two people. If your companion does not need to lower their cholesterol level then, of course, they need not eat the Special Oat Biscuit allowance for each day – just don't let them take yours!

We would also suggest that you look first at pages 158-63, our notes on the foods we use or suggest for these recipes. This will explain what they are, where they can be obtained, and how they will do you good!

Breakfast Recipes

Fruity All Bran® cereal with Apple Juice and Fresh Banana
   1 oz/30g All Bran® cereal
   2 oz/55g raisins *or* currants
   2 fl oz/60ml Plamil® soya milk concentrate
   ½ pint/285ml apple juice
   1 banana

Mix the cereal and raisins together in a breakfast bowl. Mix the milk with the same amount of cold water and pour over the cereal. Stir and serve with the juice and banana.
504 calories

Apple Porridge with Apple Juice and Fresh Banana
   1 packet instant porridge *or* 2 oz/55g porridge oats
   1 apple, cored and chopped
   1 teaspoon brown sugar
   2 fl oz/60ml Plamil® soya milk concentrate
   ½ pint/285ml apple juice
   1 banana

Prepare the porridge with the recommended amount of water, and mix in the chopped apple. Spoon into a breakfast bowl and top with the brown sugar. Pour the undiluted soya milk over the sugar. Serve hot, with apple juice and a banana.
543 calories

Easy Muesli with Grapefruit Juice

1 oz/30g rolled oats
2 oz/55g raisins *or* currants
1 apple, cored and chopped
a pinch of ground cinnamon *or* allspice
or
3 oz/85g serving of purchased muesli *without nuts*
2 fl oz/60ml Plamil® soya milk concentrate
½ pint/285ml grapefruit juice

Prepare the home-made muesli by mixing the oats, raisins, apple and spice together in a breakfast bowl. Dilute the soya milk with the same volume of cold water and pour over the cereal. Serve with the grapefruit juice.
550 calories

Speedy Fruit Bowl with Crisp Toast

10 prunes, soaked in water
8 oz/225g grapefruit segments
1 banana, sliced
2 slices crisp toast

Mix the soaked prunes and their liquid with the grapefruit segments and sliced banana. Serve with the dry toast.
NOTE: Prunes may be soaked overnight in cold water or for 20 minutes in boiling water.
528 calories

Toast and Marmite with Apple Juice, Fresh Banana and Orange

3 slices toast
1 tablespoon Marmite yeast extract (or low-salt equivalent)
½ pint/285ml apple juice
1 banana
1 orange

Prepare the toast and spread with yeast extract. Serve with apple juice, followed by the fresh banana and orange.
543 calories

Bubble 'n Squeak with Beans on Toast, Grilled Tomatoes and Grapefruit Juice

½ tablespoon Marmite yeast extract (or low-salt equivalent)
8 oz/225g mixed vegetables (frozen or leftovers)
8 oz/225g tin baked beans in tomato sauce
1 slice toast
2 tomatoes, halved
½ pint/285ml grapefruit juice

Dissolve the yeast extract in 2 fl oz/60ml warm water and pour into a large frying pan. Place over a high heat until the liquid is bubbling, then add the mixed vegetables. Turn the vegetables often with a spatula. Heat the beans and pour over the toast. Grill the tomatoes. Serve the Bubble 'n Squeak on a warm plate with the beans, toast and tomatoes. Serve with the grapefruit juice.
524 calories

Split Banana filled with Berries and 'Cream' with Crisp Toast and Grapefruit Juice

1 banana
8 oz/225g any fresh or frozen berries (i.e. strawberries, raspberries, bilberries, blackberries)
1 teaspoon sugar
2 fl oz/60ml Plamil® soya milk concentrate
2 slices crisp toast
½ pint/285ml grapefruit juice

Slice the banana in half lengthways and place open on a plate or bowl. Fill with the berries and sprinkle the sugar over them. Now pour the undiluted soya milk over the berries and serve with the dry toast and the grapefruit juice.
531 calories

Lunch Recipes

These no-fuss meals have been specially created for busy people who don't have time to prepare a large meal at lunch time. We have recommended tinned soups, for instance, as well as foods that are easy to purchase at sandwich shops, cafes and salad bars. When purchasing any of these meals, however, please make sure that they do not include 'forbidden' items such as butter, margarine, cheese or cream.

Baked Potato filled with Baked Beans or Sweetcorn and Chopped Tomato with Apple Juice

1 medium baked potato
8 oz/225g tin baked beans in tomato sauce
or
6 oz/170g tin sweetcorn, drained
1 tomato, chopped
½ pint/285ml apple juice

Fill the potato with either the heated baked beans or the sweetcorn and chopped tomato. Serve with the apple juice.
525 calores

Lentil Soup with Crackers and Marmite, Fresh Banana and Grapefruit Juice

¾ pint/425ml low-calorie tinned lentil soup
5 Ryvita or Matzo crackers
1 tablespoon Marmite yeast extract (or low-salt equivalent)
1 banana
½ pint/285ml grapefruit juice

Heat the soup and spread the crackers with the yeast extract. Serve together, followed by the banana and grapefruit juice.
526 calories

Baked Beans on Toast and Fresh Apple

1 lb/455g tin baked beans in tomato sauce
3 slices toast
1 apple

Warm the beans and pour over the toast! Follow with the apple.
563 calories

Mixed Salad Platter: Bean Salad, Green Salad and Pasta Salad

Bean salad
4 oz/115g French beans
2 oz/55g kidney beans
1 small carrot, grated
1 stalk celery, chopped
Green salad
2-3 lettuce leaves, shredded
1 tomato, chopped
5-6 slices cucumber
2 oz/55g beansprouts (i.e. alfalfa, mung)
Pasta salad
4-6 oz/115-170g cooked pasta (about 1 cupful)
1 small carrot, grated
2 oz/55g beansprouts

Serve these salads together on a large plate with a dressing of lemon juice or oil-free vinaigrette.
NOTE: These salads are available in similar form in most salad bars. If you are buying this lunch, just be certain that the salads contain no egg, fish, meat or cheese and do not add an oil-based dressing. This amount of salad should weigh approximately 1 lb/455g and fill a normal-sized plate.
525 calories

Hummus Sandwich or Pitta with Green Salad, Fresh Orange and Apple Juice

1 pitta or 2 slices bread
2 oz/55g hummus
Green salad
3 lettuce leaves, sliced
2 tomatoes, chopped
2 oz/55g beansprouts (i.e. alfalfa, mung)
5-7 slices cucumber
1 orange
½ pint/285ml apple juice

Spread the bread or pitta with the hummus and fill with salad. Serve the remaining salad to one side. Finish with the orange and apple juice.
NOTE: This is available in similar form from sandwich shops and 'kebab' takeaway restaurants.
535 calories

Rice Salad with Apple Juice

8 oz/225g cooked rice
2 oz/55g tinned peas, drained
1 medium carrot, shredded
1 stalk celery, chopped
½ oz/15g fresh parsley, chopped
2 oz/55g raisins *or* currants
lemon juice
½ pint/285ml apple juice

Mix the first six ingredients together, pour a little lemon juice over and serve. Serve with the apple juice.
NOTE: This salad is available in similar form in most salad bars. If you buy yours, be certain that it contains no egg, fish, meat or cheese and do not add an oil-based dressing. This size serving will fill a large salad bowl.
548 calories

Salad Sandwiches with Fresh Banana and Apple

4 slices bread
a little mustard or yeast extract (such as Marmite)
4 lettuce leaves
2 tomatoes, sliced
8 slices cucumber
2 oz/55g beansprouts (i.e. alfalfa, mung)
1 banana
1 apple

Spread the bread with a little mustard or yeast extract. Arrange the salad ingredients on one slice and close the sandwich with the other slice of bread. You may slice the banana into rounds and add to these sandwiches for a wholesome, sweet taste. Or eat the banana with the apple, as a dessert.
NOTE: Most of the small, family-run sandwich shops will happily make these up for you – including the banana!
544 calories

Dinner Recipes

A starter of Grapefruit Segments followed by Spaghetti with Hi-Protein Tomato Sauce

8 oz/225g grapefruit segments
2½ oz/70g raw spaghetti
½ tablespoon Marmite yeast extract (or low-salt equivalent)
1 medium onion, peeled and chopped
½ sachet/64g Protoveg TVP mince (or equivalent)
1lb/455g tin chopped tomatoes
½ teaspoon dried oregano
½ teaspoon dried basil
freshly ground black pepper to taste

Serve the grapefruit as starter or dessert.

Place a pot of water over a high heat and bring it to a boil. Add the raw spaghetti and boil for 10-12 minutes, until tender. Dissolve the yeast extract in 2 fl oz/60ml warm water and pour into a large frying pan. When the liquid bubbles, add the onion and 'sauté' until tender, about 3 minutes. Add the remaining ingredients and stir well over a medium heat, adding a little more water if necessary to make a sauce of the thickness you desire. Serve over the cooked spaghetti. Total preparation time: 25 minutes.
561 calories

A starter of Melon followed by Bean and Cauliflower Curry over Rice

1 wedge of melon (i.e. cantaloupe or honeydew)
4 oz/115g rice
½ tablespoon Marmite yeast extract (or low-salt equivalent)
1 medium onion, peeled and chopped
2 teaspoons curry powder
4 oz/115g cauliflower, chopped
8 oz/225g tin kidney beans, drained

Serve up to one-quarter of a melon as starter or dessert.

Wash the rice and place in twice its volume of water in a saucepan. Cover and simmer until the liquid is absorbed, about 20 minutes. Dissolve the yeast extract in 2 fl oz/60ml warm water, pour into a saucepan and place over a high heat. When the liquid bubbles, add the onion and 'sauté' until tender, about 3 minutes. Sprinkle the curry powder over the onion and stir well. Add the cauliflower and cook for 5 minutes, stirring often. Add the beans, stir and cover. Simmer gently for 10-15 minutes then serve over the tender rice. Total preparation time: 30 minutes.
558 calories

A starter of Green Salad followed by Easy Vegetable Casserole

Salad
4 lettuce leaves, sliced
2 tomatoes, sliced
4 slices sweet pepper
1 stalk celery, chopped
lemon juice

Casserole
1 tablespoon Marmite yeast extract (or low-salt equivalent)
1 medium onion, peeled and chopped
½ sachet/64g Protoveg TVP mince (or equivalent)
1 small potato, peeled and cubed
2 medium carrots, sliced or chopped
4 oz/115g cauliflower, chopped
4 oz/115g peas
1 teaspoon each dried thyme and parsley
freshly ground black pepper to taste
1 small potato, peeled and sliced

Arrange the salad ingredients on a plate and pour a little lemon juice over. Serve as a starter.

Pre-heat the oven to 180°C/350°F (Gas Mark 4). Dissolve the yeast extract in ½ pint/285ml warm water, pour a little into a saucepan and place over a high heat. When the liquid bubbles, add the onion and 'sauté' until tender, about 3 minutes. Add the TVP and remaining liquid and stir well. Add more water if necessary. Mix the TVP and remaining ingredients (except the sliced potato). Stir well and turn into a casserole. Arrange potato slices over the top. Cover and bake for 20 minutes, then remove the cover and bake for a further 5-10 minutes. Serve hot. Total preparation time: 40 minutes.
541 calories

A starter of Grapefruit followed by Stuffed Peppers on a bed of Rice

½ grapefruit
4 oz/115g rice
½ tablespoon Marmite yeast extract (or low-salt equivalent)
1 medium onion, peeled and chopped
½ sachet/64g Protoveg TVP mince (or equivalent)
½ oz/15g fresh parsley, chopped
½ teaspooon each dried basil and oregano
freshly ground black pepper to taste
1 large sweet pepper
8 oz/225g tin chopped tomatoes

Serve the grapefruit half as starter or dessert.

Pre-heat the oven to 180°C/350°F (Gas Mark 4). Wash the rice and place it in a saucepan and cover with twice its volume of water. Bring to the boil over a high heat, then cover and simmer for 20 minutes, or until the liquid is absorbed.

Meanwhile, dissolve the yeast extract in 2 fl oz/60ml warm water, pour this liquid into a saucepan and place over a high heat. When the liquid bubbles, add the onion and 'sauté' until the onion is tender, about 3 minutes. Add 7 fl oz/200ml water, the TVP, herbs and black pepper. Stir together and cook in the saucepan for a further 5-10 minutes, adding more liquid if necessary to make a slightly runny mixture.

Slice the sweet pepper in half lengthways, gently removing the seeds. Fill the pepper halves with the TVP mixture, place in a small baking dish and pour the chopped tomatoes over. Cover and bake for 25 minutes. Serve hot on top of the cooked rice. Total preparation time: 45 minutes.

558 calories

A starter of Tomato Soup followed by Mushroom and Lentil Pie

½ pint/285ml low-calorie tinned tomato soup
4 oz/115g raw red lentils
½ tablespoon Marmite yeast extract (or low-salt equivalent)
1 medium onion, peeled and chopped
½ teaspoon dried thyme
1 teaspoon dried parsley
freshly ground black pepper to taste
4 oz/115g mushrooms, chopped
2 small potatoes, peeled

Heat the soup and serve as a starter.

Pre-heat the oven to 180°C/350°F (Gas Mark 4). Wash and drain the lentils and cover with ½ pint/285ml water in a saucepan. Place over a high heat until the liquid begins to boil. Simmer for 15 minutes, until the lentils start to become tender. Dissolve the yeast extract in 2 fl oz/60ml warm water, pour this liquid into a saucepan and place over a high heat. When the liquid bubbles, add the onion and 'sauté' until the onion is tender, about 3 minutes. Then add the herbs, pepper and chopped mushrooms, stir well and leave to sauté over a medium heat while you prepare the potatoes.

Thinly slice the potatoes and lightly oil (or use a non-stick) casserole dish. Mix the lentils and sauté together, then pour the lentil and mushroom mixture into the casserole. Arrange the potato slices over the top of the dish. Cover the dish and bake for 30

minutes. Uncover and bake for a further 10 minutes. Serve on a warmed plate. Total preparation time: 1 hour.
528 calories

A starter of Raw Vegetable Crudités followed by Macaroni Bean Bake

Crudités
2 lettuce leaves
1 tomato, cut into wedges
4 sticks cucumber
4 sticks carrot
4 sticks (1 stalk) celery
6 radishes, trimmed
a little lemon juice
Bean Bake
3 oz/85g raw macaroni
1 medium onion, peeled and chopped
4 oz/115g French beans, frozen or tinned
4 oz/115g sweetcorn, frozen or tinned, drained
8 oz/225g tin chopped tomatoes
½ oz/15g fresh parsley, chopped
freshly ground black pepper to taste

Arrange the crudité vegetables on a plate in an attractive manner and pour a little lemon juice over. Serve as a starter.

Pre-heat the oven to 180°C/350°F (Gas Mark 4). Bring a pot of water to a boil and cook the macaroni for 7-8 minutes, until nearly tender. Drain. Mix the remaining ingredients together with the par-boiled macaroni and turn the whole mixture into a non-stick or lightly oiled casserole dish. Cover the dish and bake for 30 minutes. Serve hot. Total preparation time: 45 minutes.
529 calories

A starter of Fresh Berries followed by Sweet 'n Sour 'Pork' over Rice

4 oz/115g *any* fresh or frozen berries (i.e. raspberries, blackberries, bilberries, strawberries)
½ sachet/64g Protoveg TVP chunks (or equivalent)
4 oz/115g rice
1 medium onion, peeled and chopped
4 oz/115g carrots, sliced
4 oz/115g tin pineapple chunks, in water or juice
1 medium green pepper, seeded and coarsely chopped
2 tablespoons cider vinegar

Serve the berries in a bowl as starter or dessert

Place the TVP chunks in a bowl, cover with boiling water and leave to soak. Wash the rice and cover with twice its volume of water in a saucepan. Place over a high heat and bring to a boil. Reduce the heat, cover and simmer for 20 minutes, until the liquid is absorbed.

Heat 2 fl oz/60ml water in a large frying pan until it begins to bubble. Add the onion and carrot and 'sauté' over a high heat until tender. Drain the TVP chunks. Add the tender TVP and pineapple chunks (with their juice), cover the pan and continue to cook over a medium heat, stirring occasionally. When the TVP is soft, add the green pepper and vinegar. Simmer uncovered for 5 minutes, stirring occasionally. Serve hot over the tender rice.

576 calories

Special Oat Biscuits

In addition to eating three meals, you should eat twelve of the Special Oat Biscuits *per day* while following the Quick Cholesterol Clean-Out (for your information, this comes to about 488 calories). These biscuits provide you with a steady supply of the soluble fibre which can continue a reduction of your blood cholesterol level.

We recommend that you prepare your favourite version of the Oat Biscuits (see the instructions which follow) and then use them as snacks and 'gap fillers' throughout the day. Most people find it no trouble at all to eat biscuits in this way and many find that having a snack-like addition to their diet keeps them from 'going off the rails' and breaking their diet. For instance, if you're the sort of person who arrives home from work with nothing on your mind but eating . . . . Well, go ahead! Just make sure that you eat two or three Special Oat Biscuits. You will feel instantly full yet you won't suffer the guilt and agony of backsliding and breaking your diet. When you have fulfilled this quite natural craving, you can go ahead and prepare the evening meal you have selected.

You may have guessed that the Special Oat Biscuits are made with oat bran, one of the foods mentioned earlier which has a powerful cholesterol-lowering effect. If you recall, this is because it is high in soluble fibre of a viscous, or gluey, nature. Oat bran is on sale in most supermarkets and health-food shops. However, we found that some manufacturers package it under the label 'Oat Bran and Oat Germ' and, to begin with, we found this very confusing. In fact, 'Oat Bran' and 'Oat Bran and Oat Germ' are one and the same product! Let us explain.

When you buy wheat germ and wheat bran, you buy two different products. Wheat germ is pale yellow and rich in flavour and nutrients. Wheat bran is brown, flakey and almost pure insoluble fibre. Both are derived from the wheat milling process which easily separates the wheat grain into bran, germ and flour. With the oat grain, however, this separation of bran and germ is not possible. The bulk of the oat grain may be separated from the bran and germ, as it is for wheat, but the oat bran and oat germ remain steadfastly together. It is simply a characteristic of the oat grain. So when you go to purchase your supply of oat bran, but see only 'Oat Bran and Oat Germ' on the shelves, buy it! It is the high-soluble fibre food we are recommending.

Special Oat Biscuits are quick and easy to make at home in an oven or microwave. They do not rise and, because they are made from oat bran, they do not brown in the same way wheat-flour biscuits do. Each recipe, below, will make 24 Special Oat Biscuits, so you need only bake once every other day – keeping the cooked biscuits for up to two days in an airtight container. Alternatively, you may bake one week's supply at the weekend and freeze them in twelve-biscuit packs. This method will allow you to experiment with the various flavours and additions also listed below.

The Special Oat Biscuits Recipe

8 oz/225g packet oat bran
3 teaspoons egg replacer (see page 159)
2 teaspoons low-salt baking powder
1½ tablespoons olive oil
½ pint/285ml water

Pre-heat the oven to 180°C/350°F (Gas Mark 4) and lightly oil two baking trays or use non-stick trays. Put the oat bran into a mixing bowl. Add the egg replacer and baking powder and stir the mixture with a wooden spoon.

Add the olive oil to the dry mix and use the spoon to work it to an even, crumbly consistency. (NOTE: We recommend you use a cold-pressed olive oil. Though more expensive than many other oils, it is very nutritious, much more tasty, and since you'll use less, isn't so very expensive.)

Add the water and stir the mixture five or six times, until it is just moist. Leave the mixture to sit for 2-3 minutes, without stirring, to let it absorb the liquid.

Stir the biscuit mixture two or three times more to ensure an even absorption of liquid, then use a spoon to drop 24 walnut-sized portions of dough on to the baking trays.

Press each portion of dough flat using a flat-bottomed glass that has been dipped in water. The water will prevent the dough from sticking to the glass. Dip the glass in water after pressing each biscuit.

Place the flattened biscuits in the hot oven and bake for 12-14 minutes, depending on the efficiency of your oven. Remember that these biscuits do not brown in the same way that wheat-flour biscuits do, so be sure you do not over-cook them.

Remove the biscuits from the oven and use a spatula to lift them on to a wire rack to cool. Store in a cool, dry container for two days, or freeze immediately they have cooled.

Variations

The instructions given above will make a very plain oat biscuit which is, even so, very agreeable to many people. However, if you wish to experiment with sweet, savoury and flavoured biscuits, here are a few ideas and methods to achieve variety without affecting the effectiveness of the biscuits in lowering your cholesterol.

- Dip the moistened glass into a saucer containing 1 tablespoon brown sugar. Now when you press the biscuit dough flat, the top of the biscuit retains a thin coating of sugar. Dip the glass into the sugar before each biscuit is pressed. You many find this version very pleasing for your breakfast or after-dinner biscuits.

- Dip the moistened glass into a saucer containing 1 tablespoon crushed sesame seeds. Continue as above. This makes a nutty, wholesome flavoured biscuit that is appealing at all meal times.

- A savoury biscuit can be made by adding 1 tablespoon dried chives to the dry mixture. Prepare in the same way as for the basic biscuit, but add an extra tablespoon water. Flatten the biscuits with a wet glass.

- Other savoury variations are achieved by adding any of the following to the basic mixture: ½ teaspoon garlic granules; 1 teaspoon onion flakes; 1 teaspoon mixed sweet herbs (dried); ½ teaspoon ground cinnamon or allspice; 1 teaspoon caraway seeds. None of these versions require the addition of extra water. Flatten these biscuits with a wet glass.

- Ginger biscuits may be made adding ¾ teaspoon ground ginger to the dry mix and dissolving 1 tablespoon molasses in the ½ pint/285ml water used to moisten the oat bran. Prepare in the usual way and flatten with a wet glass.

- Any of the pure flavourings or natural essences may be added to the water before stirring into the dry mix. Try vanilla, almond or orange for a rather exotic biscuit.

Of course, you may find other variations that please you and yet do not add additional fat or cholesterol to your diet. Herbs and spices provide a great number of possibilities for you to experiment with.

A SUPPLEMENT

Once upon a time, it was no doubt possible to gather your salad vegetables from the kitchen garden minutes before you wished to use them. In this long-ago time, you wouldn't have felt the need to wonder how much pesticide residue your lettuce contained or how much Vitamin C your potatoes had lost during transport. Sadly, those carefree days are gone, to be replaced with an atmosphere of concern and misinformation about the value and quality of our daily food stuffs. In order to safeguard your health and 'insure' against the low-nutrient food we all seem likely to consume, you may wish to take a high-quality vitamin and mineral supplement on a daily basis.

Using a multi-vitamin and mineral preparation is a precaution which more and more people are taking these days, and we suggest you might like to as well, at least while you're eating a restricted diet. Should you decide on this measure, we recommend the multi-vitamin and mineral 'Cantamega 2000' (see Glossary 9).

A SIX-WEEK STRETCH

Before we go into some more detailed explanations of certain aspects of the Quick Cholesterol Clean-Out, we would like to summarize exactly what the diet entails and why it is designed the way it is.

To follow The Quick Cholesterol Clean-Out you should:
- Eat twelve Special Oat Biscuits each day without fail.
- Eat three meals per day, choosing one meal from each of the Breakfast, Lunch and Dinner selections listed above.
- Follow the diet for about six weeks then check your progress.

You can see that the diet is easy to understand and easy to follow. The meals are quick to prepare and many are available in canteens, sandwich bars and restaurants, making working lunches especially convenient.

We recommend that you follow the diet for six weeks. Medical trials of various cholesterol-reducing diets have been conducted for periods of time ranging from seven days to several years, with some results indicating that measureable reductions in blood cholesterol are achievable in as little as *ten days*. However, we suggest that an initial six-week period will allow you to check your progress and get an idea of what you can achieve. When you have your cholesterol level tested at the end of the six-week diet period, you may compare it to your initial test and see for yourself the percentage reduction you have attained. People respond differently to different substances, so it is impossible to predict how you personally will respond. However, scientific studies have shown that eating 100g oat bran a day – which is roughly how much there is in twelve Special Oat Biscuits – often produces a total cholesterol reduction in the region of 10-25 per cent, probably depending to some extent on the degree of elevation of serum cholesterol to begin with, and whether a low-fat diet is also being consumed at the same time. More about this in Chapter Six.

We have found that six weeks is sufficient time for new culinary and dietary habits to become established. Habit is a powerful force in most people's lives, and wields its power in most aspects of life. You probably live much of each day in a habitual way: what you wear, what you eat, how you cook it, how you travel, work and sleep. You might perform these activities in the way you do simply because you have performed them in that way for a very long time. That is a characteristic of habit. Habit is a way of doing something that means you don't give as much thought to it as you once did, a sort of 'running on automatic' that everyone does to a greater or lesser extent. In many situations, habit is a real blessing: most of us would rather not think really hard about how to brush our teeth. We would rather think of something more stimulating while brushing our teeth automatically, out of habit.

Habit, by itself, is neither good nor bad; yet there can be good and bad habits so it is always valuable to run a check on your own set of habits to make sure they are worth keeping. Certainly the food we eat and the way we prepare it are habit-prone areas of our lives which need to be reappraised from time to time to determine whether or not they are habits we benefit from.

During the six weeks you follow the Quick Cholesterol Clean-Out, you will probably be robbed of several old food habits. This is the part of any diet programme that makes people feel like cheating, quitting or never starting in the first place. But stop right there. The foods and cookery methods you feel so attached to are only *habits* that you have been lugging round for years! We recommend that you follow this diet for six weeks because we want you to establish a *new* set of food habits. It will give you time to develop new ways of thinking about the food you eat, new ways of selecting and preparing it and, hopefully, a whole new, enhanced state of health as a result.

IN CASE OF EMERGENCY

When you're tempted to break the diet (and you will be, you know!) we'd like you to read this section very carefully. First, if you're simply feeling hungry, then go ahead and eat a little more.

Although you may find that you lose some weight on the Quick Cholesterol Clean-Out, that's not really the intention of the diet – for many people, however, it *will* be a beneficial side-effect. Hunger pangs can be eased simply by serving yourself slightly larger portions, or, alternatively, by adding 'Extra Calorie Foods' from the recipes that follow. However, the people who tested our diet found that hunger never happened. They found themselves eating *smaller* portions than listed.

If you are tempted by a friend or colleague to 'go on, just one little binge won't hurt' you must be strong and tell them that it *will* hurt, very much indeed. Firstly, we have found that cholesterol reduction occurs most efficiently when dietary cholesterol is *eliminated*. If you still eat even a little, your rate of reduction will be slowed. And secondly, you must try to change your taste preferences (something which will naturally start to happen over six weeks) to appreciate new food. A 'binge' is bad because it tells your body to go back to the old ways of thinking about food. If you cheat on the diet, you're just cheating yourself. It's as simple as that.

We have found that many people can control their diets with ease – until they are invited out to a meal. It seems that restaurants, in particular, are difficult places in which to follow a diet. We hope to make it slightly easier for you by offering a few tips.

● Pick the type of restaurant you visit. It wouldn't make much sense to go to a steak-house when you are on a cholesterol-reducing diet, would it? Try a good Italian, Chinese or Mediterranean restaurant instead. They *always* have rice, bean, pasta and vegetable dishes on their menus so it won't be so difficult for you to come up with a suitable meal. Nevertheless, try to reserve eating-out for treats only.

● Other types of restaurant, such as Mexican or French, should be able to offer you a large, freshly made salad (insist on it being fresh) or an attractive platter of in-season vegetables with a special low-fat sauce. Fresh fruit is always available as a starter or dessert. If you want to be sure a suitable meal will be offered, ring ahead and talk to the chef. Any chef worth his or her title should be skilled enough, and interested enough in your contentment, to make you a meal you can eat. If it seems likely that you won't have a pleasant meal, use your trump card and go somewhere else!

● Eating out at the home of friends or relations is a different matter because, hopefully, they will be interested in your diet and want to help you succeed. We suggest you simply talk your diet through with them at some point before they do their shopping. If they are at all interested in 'ethnic' or vegetarian cookery, they will have no trouble and probably lots of fun preparing a meal you can all enjoy and benefit from.

● Quick snacks or 'bites' of lunch are available – without ruining your success – from most salad bars, sandwich shops and cafes selling baked potatoes. Just be sure to avoid high-fat dressings and fillings!

And do try using the following little note which will prove useful to you in a variety of social settings – copy it and use it when you need to. Most people will find it intriguing, and it will probably spark off an interesting conversation anywhere. The rest is up to you!

I'm doing the 'Quick Cholesterol Clean-Out' at the moment, and need your help to stay on the straight and narrow. Here is a list of foods that will bring me success, and another list of those that I don't wish to eat at the moment. Please use any of the foods in the left-hand column, and **avoid** *those in the right-hand column when preparing my meal. Thank you for your help.*

YES, Please!	NO, Thank You
Fruit	Meat and Poultry
Vegetables	Shell Fish
Grain	Eggs
Beans	Cheese
Pulses	Milk and Cream
Olive oil	All types of animal fats

Obviously, it is wise to plan the starting date of your diet so that it doesn't coincide with the middle of your holiday abroad or with Christmas. That precaution apart, we find that there is very little else that cannot be adjusted to accommodate the Quick Cholesterol Clean-Out. If you're pleased with your diet, do write and tell us. There's an address at the end of this book, and we'd love to know how you get on!

NEED EXTRA CALORIES?

There are some people, mostly men leading an active life, who need more calories per day than these menus provide. For example, a man who takes daily exercise may require up to 3000 calories per day, about 800 calories more than provided in each of these menus. A very active man, one whose job involves heavy physical labour, for instance, may require a further 200-500 calories more than this to make a grand total of up to 3500 calories per day! For these people we include a number of meal suggestions and recipes that will boost your calorie intake.

An easy way to boost your daily intake by an extra 1000 calories (from 2200 to 3200) is to add another one-half portion of each dish to your meals. For instance, a breakfast of All Bran® is listed as 1 oz/30g per person which you could easily change to a 1½ oz/45g serving for yourself. Similarly, a lunch of two Club Sandwiches could very easily become three sandwiches, and when the meal consists largely of a salad, simply eat as much as you like.

If you don't want to add quite as many extra calories as that, you may use some of the following extra-calorie foods to boost your intake. These may be eaten at meal times, or during your mid-morning or mid-afternoon snack. Please note that if you decide to increase your calorie intake, you do not need to increase the number of Oat Biscuits you eat each day – twelve is still the optimum number.

Baked Beans in Tomato sauce
290 calories in a 1lb/455g tin. Also high in fibre, protein, folacin, Vitamin B6, niacin, potassium, iron and zinc. Try to purchase low-salt varieties.

Baked Potato
220 calories in a medium potato. Also rich in Vitamins C and B6 and in potassium and iron. Do not add butter, margarine, soured cream, mayonnaise or other dairy-based dressings, but add any amount of salad.

Bread and Toast
Cracked wheat or granary: 66 calories in one slice.
Rye: 61 calories in one slice.
White, wheat flour: 63 calories in one slice.
Whole-Wheat: 67 calories in one slice.

Coffee Substitute
9 calories in 1 teaspoon of the mixture. Dilute with 6 fl oz/170ml boiling water.

Crackers or Biscuits
Matzos: 17 calories in each.
Water biscuits (unsalted): 12 calories in each.
Wheat Thins: 9 calories in each.

Fruit

Apple, raw: 81 calories in one of medium size.
Apple, dried: 105 calories in 4 oz/115g.
Apple sauce, unsweetened: 53 calories in 4 oz/115g.
Apricot, raw: 20 calories in one of medium size.
Apricot, dried: 155 calories in 4 oz/115g.
Banana: 105 calories in one of medium size.
Blackberries: 74 calories in 8 oz/225g.
Cherries: 77 calories in 8 oz/225g.
Currants, dried: 203 calories in 4 oz/115g.
Dates, fresh or dried: 228 calories in 10 fruits (about 4 oz/115g).
Fig, dried: 254 calories in 10 fruits (about 4 oz/115g.)
Fig, raw: 37 calories each.
Grape, raw: 36 calories in 10 fruits.
Grapefruit: 46 calories per fruit.
Kiwi, raw: 46 calories each.
Mango, raw: 108 calories in one large fruit.
Melon
  Cantaloupe: 94 calories per half melon.
  Honeydew: 46 calories per slice (about one-eighth of melon).
  Watermelon: 50 calories in an 8 oz/225g slice.
Nectarine, raw: 67 calories each.
Orange, raw: 65 calories each.
Peach, dried: 192 calories per 4 oz/115g.
Peach, raw: 37 calories each.
Pear, dried: 236 calories per 4 oz/115g.
Pear, raw: 98 calories each.
Pineapple, fresh: 77 calories per 2-3 slices (about 8 oz/225g).
Plum, raw: 36 calories each.
Pomegranate, raw: 104 calories each.
Prunes: 200 calories per 10 fruits.
Raisins: 247 calories per 4 oz/115g.
Raspberries, fresh: 61 calories per 8 oz/225g.
Rhubarb, fresh: 26 calories per 8 oz/225g.
Strawberries: 45 calories per 8 oz/225g.
Tangerine, raw: 37 calories each.

Fruit Juices: per ½ pint/285ml serving, unsweetened
Apple: 145 calories.
Grape: 193 calories.
Grapefruit: 116 calories.
Orange: 139 calories.
Pineapple: 174 calories.
Prune: 114 calories.
Lemon and Lime: 4 calories per tablespoon.

Hummus
210 calories in 4 oz/115g. Also considered a high-fat food so use very sparingly. Rich in folacin, Vitamin B6 and iron.

Jams and Preserves
54 calories in 1 tablespoon. Choose sugar-free jams or pure fruit spreads if possible.

Pasta
192 calories in 8 oz/225g cooked pasta, any sort.

Popcorn
23 calories in 1 breakfast bowlful (cooked without oil).
41 calories in 1 breakfast bowlful (cooked with oil).

Rice
232 calories in 8 oz/225g cooked brown rice.
223 calories in 8 oz/225g cooked white rice.

Sandwiches
183 calories in one Salad Sandwich to the following recipe:
2 slices whole-wheat bread spread with 1 teaspoon prepared mustard.
Fill with 2 lettuce leaves, 8 slices cucumber, 1 sliced tomato and a small handful of alfalfa (or other bean) sprouts.
269 calories in a Tofu Salad Sandwich – as above, but add 4 oz/115g sliced tofu strips.

Scone
105 calories in one of medium size, without raisins. Please use olive oil if making your own. Do not serve with butter or margarine, though a little jam may be served.

Soups
Gazpacho: 70 calories in ½ pint/285ml.
Lentil: 145 calories in ½ pint/285ml.
Onion: 70 calories in ½ pint/285 ml.
Tomato: 230 calories in 12 fl oz/340ml.
Vegetable: 90 calories in ½ pint/285ml.
NOTE: Please select soups made with vegetable stock.

Vegetable Burger
200 calories for a 3-4 oz/115g burger.
NOTE: Please select those that may be baked or grilled, not fried.

Vegetables
Artichoke, Globe: 53 calories in 1 of medium size, boiled.
Asparagus: 15 calories in 4 cooked spears.
Beetroot, pickled: 75 calories in 4 oz/115g.
Pumpkin, tinned: 154 calories in 1lb/455g tin.
Sauerkraut, tinned: 85 calories in 1lb/455g tin.
Sweet potato, baked: 233 calories in 8 oz/225g.
NOTE: These are the more unusual vegetables that you might prepare occasionally, rather than on a daily basis. Most other vegetables are listed below under 'Free Foods'.

Vegetable Juices: per ½ pint/285ml serving
Carrot: 112 calories.
Tomato: 48 calories.
Vegetable Juice Cocktail: 53 calories.

Vinaigrette
35 calories in the following recipe:
¼ pint/140ml cider vinegar mixed with 2 teaspoons prepared mustard, chopped garlic, black pepper and dried herbs to taste.

FREE FOODS

These foods normally contain no more than 25 calories per serving, where a serving weighs approximately 4 oz/115g. They do not contain any cholesterol. When fresh, these foods are usually rich in vitamins, minerals and fibre. Therefore, you may enjoy as much of these foods as you like, over and above your day's diet, without worrying about excess calories, cholesterol or fat.

Please note that when a food is cooked, the cooking method must not include fat. Steaming, grilling, baking or other non-fat methods should be used instead.

Fruit
Currants, red or black
Gooseberries
Grapefruit, one-half
Lemon
Lime
Melon – such as canteloupe, honeydew, watermelon
Raspberries
Rhubarb
Strawberries

Vegetables

Artichokes, globe
Asparagus, 4 spears
Aubergine
Beansprouts (such as alfalfa
    or mung)
Broccoli
Brussels sprouts
Cabbage
Carrots
Cauliflower
Celery
Courgettes
Cress
Cucumber

Leeks
Lettuce
Marrow
Mushrooms
Okra (Ladies' Finger)
Onions
Radishes
Runner beans
Spinach
Swede
Sweet pepper
Tomatoes
Turnip
Watercress

ADDITIONAL RECIPES

These recipes may be used to provide variety and extra substance
to your diet. They are especially useful for those who need more
than 2200 calories per day.

Bubble and Squeak

    1 medium potato, peeled and cooked
    8 oz/225g vegetables (such as Brussels sprouts, carrots, peas),
        cooked
    ½ tablespoon Marmite yeast extract (or low-salt equivalent)
        dissolved in 2 fl oz/60ml warm water

Chop the vegetables. Pour the yeast extract liquid into a large
frying pan and place over a high heat. When the liquid begins to
bubble, add the chopped vegetables and 'sauté' for 5-7 minutes.
Use a spatula to turn the mixture three or four times during cooking. Serve hot.
200 calories

Pasta with Vegetable Sauce
This is a filling and substantial dish that is very quick to prepare. If you like, you may use whatever vegetables you have in stock to make this a real 'pot-luck' dish.

Ingredients per person
   2½ oz/70g uncooked pasta, any eggless variety
   2 medium tomatoes, chopped
   1 small onion, peeled and chopped
   1 clove garlic, chopped (optional)
   4 oz/115g any raw or cooked vegetable, chopped
   ½ teaspoon dried oregano
   ½ teaspoon dried basil
   freshly gound black pepper to taste

Bring a pot of water to a rapid boil and add the pasta. Boil for 10-12 minutes, until just tender.

Place the chopped tomatoes in a frying pan over a medium heat. Stir frequently until the liquid begins to bubble. Add the onion and garlic and stir frequently until soft. Add the remaining ingredients, stir well and leave to cook for 10-15 minutes, stirring occasionally. Add a little water if necessary.

Drain the pasta, serve on to a warmed plate and spoon the sauce over. Serve immediately.
380 calories

Apple Sauce
This keeps for a week in a jar placed in the refrigerator. It is very low in calories because no sugar is added. Try it instead of jam or preserves, or as a sauce with some of the hot dishes.

   2lb/900g cooking apples, washed and chopped
   juice of 2 lemons
   ½-1 teaspoon ground cinnamon
   1 teaspoon pectin powder, optional

Place the chopped apples in a deep saucepan over a medium heat. Do not discard the apple cores or skin, but add them to the pan as well. Add the lemon juice to the apples and stir occasionally while they cook. Gradually the apples will become mushy and, at this stage, you may add the ground cinnamon and pectin. Stir often as the apples turn into a sauce, about 30 minutes in total, then press the mixture through a sieve to remove the seeds and skin. Serve immediately or seal and keep in a jar in the refrigerator.
566 calories

Oat Cakes

The raisins add a slight sweetness to these little cakes. You may eat half this amount instead of your Oat Biscuits if you like, but they are higher in calories – make sure you can afford it!

- 8 oz/225g oat bran
- 2 teaspoons baking powder
- 3 teaspoons egg replacer
- 4 oz/115g raisins
- 2 tablespoons olive oil
- ½ pint/285ml water

Pre-heat the oven to 180°C/350°F (Gas Mark 4). Mix the dry ingredients and the raisins together in a bowl. Add the olive oil and work it into the dry mix to create an even, crumbly texture. Add the water and stir three or four times until the mixture is just moistened. Leave to sit for 2-3 minutes.

Line twelve to fifteen small cake tins with paper baking cases. Stir the mixture once or twice more, then spoon it into the baking cases. Bake for 15-17 minutes. Cool before serving.

NOTE: These cakes do not brown in the same way that wheat-flour cakes do. Therefore, be certain not to overcook.

1260 calories (84-105 calories per cake)

Special Date and Spice Cakes

These are delicious, sweet and spicy cakes with an irresistible texture. Kids and family will love them. Substitute half of this amount for your daily quota of Oat Biscuits but remember they are high in calories so this swap should only be done occasionally.

- 4 oz/115g rolled oats
- 4¼ oz/125g oat bran
- 2 teaspoons baking powder
- 3 teaspoons egg replacer
- ½ teaspoon ground cinnamon
- 4 oz/115g chopped dates
- 2 tablespoons olive oil
- ½ pint/285ml water

Pre-heat the oven to 180°C/350°F (Gas Mark 4). Mix the first five ingredients together in a large bowl. Add the dates and oil and work to an even, crumbly consistency. Now add the water, stir two or three times and leave to sit for 2-3 minutes.

Line sixteen to twenty small cake tins with paper baking cases. Spoon the cake mixture into them to about three-quarters of their depth. Bake for 15 minutes. Cool before serving.

1425 calories (72-90 calories per cake)

5
THE LOW-CHOLESTEROL GOURMET

High serum cholesterol is not a male-only or female-only disorder and we felt that many spouses and partners might wish to follow the Quick Cholesterol Clean-Out together. So we designed the Low-Cholesterol Gourmet which is intended to serve two people – in style! Here is a collection of ten menus which each describe a whole day's food. And because more and more people – men and women alike – are increasingly interested in cooking, we decided to make these menus slightly more . . . well, exciting. Of course, they're still easy to make and quite convenient, too; it's just that a little more creative energy is involved in preparing these feasts.

If you are following the diet alone, but are attracted by the menus listed here then, by all means try them! Simply halve each recipe, or eat the same menu two days in a row, or freeze half of each recipe immediately after you make it.

WE AIM TO PLEASE

We would like you to enjoy your meals as much as possible, so we have created themes for each day's menu to help build the character and flavours of the dishes described. Please choose each day's menu from those provided, selecting menus in any order you like. We have found that one's mood, the day of the week and even one's work load will affect the type of menu which appeals. Please indulge yourself and select the menu that will make you most satisfied today! If you like the sound of all ten menus, then you need only repeat each one four times during the six-week diet period. That is more variety than most people get in their meals!

No Mixing This Time
If you don't have time to follow a Gourmet menu on any given day, then go back to Chapter Four and prepare your meals by choosing one from each of the Breakfast, Lunch and Dinner selection listed there. You can return to the Low-Cholesterol Gourmet diet the next day, or whenever you feel like a treat. However, you mustn't choose one or two meals from that chapter and part of a menu from this. No, once you start the day in one version of the diet, you

should continue the day in that version.

You may repeat any one of these Low-Cholesterol Gourmet menus as often as you like, even ignoring those you don't like the sound of, but you should never split a menu. In other words, once you start a day's menu, you must not switch half way through the day to another menu. This would upset the nutritional profile of your diet.

Nutrition

Each of these ten menus describes a day's diet which provides meals naturally high in substances which have been shown to have a cholesterol-lowering effect. Each menu has been nutritionally analysed to ensure that you receive acceptable amounts of 'complete' protein, vitamins and minerals for each day. There are 2200 calories available in each day's menu, which is the average requirement for a woman aged 18 to 54 (women over 55 need slightly less). It is also adequate for many men who are obese, and therefore in need of a reduced-calorie diet. Most people will find these meals very filling due to their reliance on high-fibre foods. However, if you find you need more food, please give yourself bigger portions by extending the recipes by one-quarter or one-half; if you need fewer calories, just reduce the size of your portions a little. (Please see Chapter Four for information on both higher-calorie and 'free' calorie foods.) As with the Quick Cholesterol Clean-Out diet in the previous chapter, the percentage of total fats in this diet has been reduced to 20 per cent of total calories, and foods containing cholesterol have been completely avoided.

A Dozen Biscuits

In the Low-Cholesterol Gourmet diet you should aim to eat a total of twelve Special Oat Biscuits each day – just as you did in the Quick Cholesterol Clean-Out diet. The recipe for these biscuits is on page 73 and any of the variations listed there are suitable for this diet as well. Although in these menus we have suggested the numbers you should eat at specific times, you may, of course, alter this schedule to suit yourself. For instance, many people love a small snack just before bed. If this sounds like you, then simply eat any number of Special Oat Biscuits at this time! Take them from your Snack or Dinner allowance and enjoy them with a cup of warm herbal tea to send you off to sleep. The Special Oat Biscuits are an essential part of this diet because they contain that certain type of soluble fibre which has a considerable cholesterol-lowering effect. Please don't skip them!

Lunch and Learn

Many people go out to work each day and, for this reason we have attempted to create lunch recipes which are either quick to prepare the night before and easy to take to work with you, or which may be purchased in similar form from a restaurant or sandwich bar. For example, the Tabbouleh Salad in the Greek Menu can often be found in salad bars, and baked potato with baked beans (no butter or margarine!) can also be found quite easily at lunchtime. Most pre-made salad dressings should be avoided, but if you are eating out and need something to put on the salad, please ask for any amount of freshly squeezed lemon juice or an olive oil (be specific) and vinegar dressing, and be very sparing with it (less than a tablespoonful).

We know that lunch isn't the only time of day when people eat out, however. Please refer to the chart on page 78 which we have designed specially for you to photocopy and show to cooks and chefs when eating out. A good chef will find this diet very easy to prepare for, so there is no reason why you should break your diet just because you are eating away from home. And here is a short list of foods for you to watch for when the chef is your mother or best friend!

What You *Won't* Be Eating

These are the foods you *must avoid* while on this diet.

meat	fish
chicken	poultry and game
cheese	milk
butter	lard
margarine	all other animal foods

fatty and oily 'snacks' such as crisps, nuts, etc.

What You *Will* Be Eating

The good news is that all of the fruits, grains, vegetables, seeds, beans, legumes and pulses are yours to enjoy. These foods are rich in nutrients and many are high in soluble fibre, which makes them essential to this cholesterol reduction diet. In fact, the list of included foods is very long indeed, possibly several hundreds! And so that you can start eating them very soon, here are the ten menus, and their recipes, included in the Low-Cholesterol Gourmet.

THE CALIFORNIA MENU

Think of health, energy and that special spring in the step that good living brings and, chances are, you will at some point think of California. Most of the people there are genuinely interested in improving their lives where possible but, like most Americans, Californians love to eat! Fortunately, they are blessed with a climate that will allow them to eat home-grown fruit, vegetables and grains the year round so their regional diet is one that is fresh and filling. The California diet is also fun – they love trying new foods and new ways of preparing meals, like the exotic sounding Pacific Scrambled Tofu which is a delicious Los Angeles version of scrambled eggs.

Breakfast
All Bran® Cereal with Apple Juice
Pacific Scrambled Tofu
2 Oat Biscuits
Herbal Tea

Snack
3 Oat Biscuits
Mineral Water or Herbal Tea

Lunch
Baked Potato filled with Baked Beans
Fresh Orange
2 Oat Biscuits

Snack
3 Oat Biscuits
Mineral Water or Herbal Tea

Dinner
Hi-Protein Pizza with California Salad and Special Coleslaw
Baked Apple
Banana Shake
2 Oat Biscuits
Herbal Tea

California Shopping List for two people

From your greengrocer:
2 baking potatoes
2 medium onions
8 oz/225g carrots
8oz/225g cabbage
8oz/225g broccoli
2-3 small courgettes
4 oz/115g beansprouts (i.e. alfalfa, mung)
2 medium sweet peppers
4 oz/115g mushrooms
1 oz/30g fresh parsley
2 medium tomatoes
2 cloves garlic (optional)
4 lettuce leaves
1 lemon (juice of)
2 large apples
1 ripe banana
2 navel oranges

From your supermarket or health-food shop:
1 pint/570ml fresh, unsweetened apple juice
All Bran® cereal
10 oz/285g carton firm tofu
½ pint/285ml Plamil® soya milk concentrate
1lb/455g tin baked beans in tomato sauce (low-salt variety)
1 oz/30g raisins
1 oz/30g rolled oats
1 sachet/128g Protoveg TVP mince (or equivalent)
5 oz/140g tin tomato purée
6 oz/170g whole-wheat flour

And from your own cupboard:
1 tablespoon molasses
1 tablespoon Marmite yeast extract (or low-salt equivalent)
2 teaspoons prepared yellow mustard
4 tablespoons cider vinegar
½ teaspoon turmeric
2 tablespoons brewer's yeast
pinch ground nutmeg *or* allspice
pinch ground cinnamon
ground black pepper to taste
dried basil and oregano to taste

California Breakfast

All Bran® Cereal with Apple Juice
2 oz/55g All Bran® cereal
1 pint/570ml fresh, unsweetened apple juice

Measure 1oz/30g of cereal into each of two bowls. Pour ½ pint/285ml of the apple juice over each serving and stir well. Serve immediately.

Pacific Scrambled Tofu
1 medium onion, peeled and chopped
½ teaspoon turmeric
2-3 small courgettes, sliced
1 medium sweet pepper, de-seeded and chopped
10 oz/285g firm tofu, cubed
1 tablespoon brewer's yeast

Pour approximately 2 fl oz/60ml of water into a deep frying pan and place over a high heat until the water is bubbling. Add the chopped onion and stir constantly for 2-3 minutes, until it softens. Sprinkle the turmeric over the onion and stir well to ensure an even colour. Add the courgettes, and stir frequently for 5 minutes over a medium heat.

Next add the sweet pepper (red or green), the tofu and yeast and stir frequently over a medium heat. The tofu should 'scramble' and become yellow in colour; the pepper should soften. Add a little more water at this stage if the mixture is sticking to the pan, but avoid making the mixture runny. Continue to cook until the vegetables are tender and the mixture is very hot. Serve immediately in warmed bowls.

Accompaniments
2 Oat Biscuits per person
any amount of herbal tea or mineral water

California Snack
3 Oat Biscuits per person
Herbal tea *or* mineral water

California Lunch

Baked Potato filled with Baked Beans
2 large baking potatoes
1lb/455g tin baked beans in tomato sauce (low-salt variety)

Pre-heat the oven to 190°C/375°F (Gas Mark 5) while you scrub the potatoes. Pierce each potato with a metal skewer and bake in the hot oven until tender, about 35 minutes. Alternatively, bake the potatoes in a microwave according to manufacturers' instructions.

Warm the beans in a small saucepan over a low heat. When the potatoes are cooked, place one on each plate and slice each potato in half. Pour the baked beans over the open potatoes and serve immediately.

Dessert
1 fresh navel orange per person
2 Oat Biscuits per person
any amount of herbal tea or mineral water

California Snack
3 Oat Biscuits per person
Herbal tea *or* mineral water

California Dinner

Hi-Protein Pizza
6 oz/170g whole-wheat flour
1 tablespoon Marmite yeast extract (or low-salt equivalent)
Sauce
5 oz/140g tin tomato purée (low-salt)
1 tablespoon brewer's yeast
½ oz/15g fresh parsley, chopped
freshly ground black pepper to taste
1 teaspoon dried basil
½ teaspoon dried oregano
Topping
1 medium onion, peeled and finely chopped
2 cloves garlic, crushed (optional)
1 sachet/128g Protoveg TVP mince (or equivalent)
4 oz/115g mushrooms, sliced
1 medium sweet pepper, de-seeded and sliced or chopped

Pre-heat the oven to 180°C/350°F (Gas Mark 4). Measure the flour into a mixing bowl and make a well in the centre. Dissolve the yeast extract in ¼ pint/140ml warm water and pour gradually into the flour, stirring after each addition. Work to a firm dough, adding more water if necessary. Lightly oil a 12 inch/30cm baking tray or flan dish and spread the dough evenly to the edges. Use your fingers or the back of a spoon to press the dough into the corners.

Measure the tomato purée and the brewer's yeast into a saucepan and stir in ¾ pint/425ml water. Place over a medium heat and bring to a simmer. Add the fresh parsley, pepper, basil and oregano and stir well. Leave to simmer, uncovered, over a low heat until needed.

Pour 2 fl oz/60ml water into a frying pan and place over a high heat until the water bubbles. Add the onion and garlic and stir constantly while the onion softens, about 3 minutes. Add the TVP to this 'sauté', stir well and gradually add 15 fl oz/425ml water to the mixture. Continue stirring over a high heat while the TVP softens, about 5 minutes. Remove the sauce and this mixture from the heat.

Spread the TVP mixture evenly over the pizza base. Top with a thin layer of sauce, also spread evenly. Next, arrange the mushrooms and peppers over the sauce. Finally, pour the remaining sauce over the pepper. Bake the pizza for 35-40 minutes in the hot oven. Slice and serve hot or cold.

California Salad

8 oz/225g broccoli, trimmed
4 oz/115g carrots, shredded
4 oz/115g cabbage, shredded
4 lettuce leaves, thinly sliced
½ oz/15g fresh parsley, chopped
2 medium tomatoes, coarsely chopped
2 tablespoons lemon juice
freshly ground black pepper to taste

Steam the broccoli until it is just tender, then remove it from the pan and leave it to cool in the open. Cut into small pieces.

Mix the vegetables together in a large salad bowl and gently toss them together. Now pour over the lemon juice and sprinkle with pepper. Toss again and serve in two portions.

Special Coleslaw
    4 oz/115g beansprouts (i.e. alfalfa, mung)
    4 oz/115g carrots, shredded
    4 oz/115g cabbage, shredded
    Dressing
    4 tablespoons cider vinegar
    2 teaspoons prepared mustard
    2 fl oz/60ml Plamil® soya milk concentrate
    freshly ground black pepper to taste

Toss the beansprouts, carrots and cabbage together in a large bowl. Measure the ingredients for the dressing into a jug or jar and shake or stir them together. Pour the dressing over the vegetables and toss the coleslaw. Divide into two portions and serve.

Baked Apple
    2 large apples
    1oz/30g raisins
    1 oz/30g rolled oats
    1 tablespoon molasses
    pinch ground cinnamon

Pre-heat the oven to 170°C/325°F (Gas Mark 3). Wash and carefully core the apples, making sure the apples do not split in half. Place them side by side in a small casserole dish.

Mix the remaining ingredients together in a bowl. Press half this mixture into the hollow centre of each apple. Cover the dish and bake the apples for 30-40 minutes (while you eat dinner!). If a slight crust is desired, uncover the casserole for the last 5-10 minutes. Serve hot. If you wish, pour a tablespoon of Plamil® soya milk concentrate over each apple.

Banana Shake
    8 fl oz/225ml Plamil® soya milk concentrate
    ¼ pint/140ml cold water
    1 ripe banana
    pinch ground nutmeg *or* allspice

Dilute the soya milk with the water and pour into a food blender. Break the banana into small pieces and add to the milk. Add the spice and purée the mixture to a thick, even consistency. Pour into two glasses and serve, cold if possible.

Accompaniments
2 Oat Biscuits per person
Herbal tea

CARIBBEAN MENU

Just thinking about the fruits and exotic vegetables used in Caribbean cooking is enough to make most people rush into the kitchen and make a meal. Influences from Africa, Spain, France and India have built a wonderful variety into Caribbean cuisine, which is as visually attractive as it is flavourful. This menu does the best it can in a country that doesn't enjoy the sun-kissed beaches and avocado trees of the West Indies. We find the breakfast particularly refreshing, while the Marinade Salad provides a real picnic-style lunch that can be made in large quantity and stored in the refrigerator for three to four days.

Breakfast
Melon filled with Lemon Figs and Sliced Banana
All Bran® Cereal with Plamil®
2 Oat Biscuits
Herbal Tea

Snack
3 Oat Biscuits
Mineral Water or Herbal Tea

Lunch
Marinade Salad
2 Oat Biscuits
Herbal Tea or Mineral Water

Snack
3 Oat Biscuits
Mineral Water or Herbal Tea

Dinner
Carrot and Kidney Bean Ragout over Parsley Rice
Grilled Grapefruit
2 Oat Biscuits
Herbal Tea

Caribbean Shopping List for two people

From your greengrocer:
2 medium onions
1 lb/455g carrots
1 lb/455g French beans
1 medium sweet pepper
8 oz/225g cabbage
1 lb/455g broccoli
4 oz/115g mushrooms
1 oz/30g fresh parsley
3 cloves garlic (optional)
1 large grapefruit
1 whole melon (honeydew or cantaloupe)
4 oz/115g dried figs
2 bananas
2 lemons (juice of)

From your supermarket or health-food shop:
All Bran® cereal
½ pint /285ml Plamil® soya milk concentrate
4 oz/115g rice
½ pint/285ml cider vinegar
1 lb/455g tin kidney beans (low-salt)
1 sachet/128g Protoveg TVP chunks (or equivalent)

And from your own cupboard:
1 tablespoon Marmite yeast extract (or low-salt equivalent)
1 tablespoon brown sugar
ground black pepper
mustard seed
ground or whole cloves
bay leaf

Caribbean Breakfast

Melon filled with Lemon Figs and Sliced Banana
    1 whole melon (honeydew or cantaloupe), sliced in half
    4 oz/115g dried figs, washed and chopped
    2 bananas, sliced
    3 tablespoons lemon juice

Clean the seeds from the middle of each melon half and discard them. Place the chopped figs and bananas together in a mixing bowl, pour over the lemon juice and stir well. Spoon half of this mixture into each of the melon halves and serve.

All Bran® Cereal with Plamil®
2 oz/55g All Bran® cereal
½ pint/285ml Plamil soya milk concentrate

Measure 1oz/30g of cereal into each of two bowls. Add ¼ pint/140ml cold water to the soya milk and stir well. Pour half of the diluted soya milk over each serving and stir well. Serve immediately.

Accompaniments
2 Oat Biscuits per person
Herbal tea

Caribbean Snack
3 Oat Biscuits per person
Mineral water *or* herbal tea

Caribbean Lunch

Marinade Salad
1 lb/455g broccoli, trimmed
1 lb/455g French beans, fresh or tinned
8 oz/225g cabbage, shredded
1 medium sweet pepper, de-seeded and chopped
½ oz/15g fresh parsley, chopped
Marinade
½ pint/285ml cider vinegar
1 teaspoon mustard seed
freshly ground black pepper to taste
1 bay leaf

Coarsely chop the broccoli and beans and prepare the remaining vegetables. In a large enamel saucepan, heat the vinegar to a very gentle simmer. Add the mustard seed, pepper and bay leaf and leave the marinade to simmer, covered, for 2-3 minutes. Add the broccoli and beans to the marinade, stir well and simmer, covered, for 7-10 minutes. Add the remaining vegetables, stir, cover the pan and remove from the heat.

Leave the pan covered and allow the marinade to cool. Then place in an airtight container and chill until ready to serve.
NOTE: This dish improves in flavour and texture from standing overnight.

Accompaniments
2 Oat Biscuits per person
Herbal tea *or* mineral water

Caribbean Snack
3 Oat Biscuits per person
Mineral water *or* herbal tea

Caribbean Dinner

Carrot and Kidney Bean Ragoût over Parsley Rice
4 oz/115g rice
1 tablespoon Marmite yeast extract (or low-salt equivalent)
2 medium onions, peeled and chopped
3 cloves garlic, crushed (optional)
1 sachet /128g Protoveg TVP chunks (or equivalent)
1 lb/455g carrots, sliced into rounds
1 lb/455g tin kidney beans (low-salt variety), drained
4 oz/115g mushrooms, quartered
¼ teaspoon ground cloves *or* 6 whole cloves
1 bay leaf
freshly ground black pepper to taste
½ oz/15g fresh parsley, chopped

· Rinse the rice, place in a deep saucepan and cover with twice its volume of cold water. Place over a high heat until the liquid comes to a boil. Stir once, then cover the pan and reduce the heat. Leave the rice to simmer, undisturbed, for 25 minutes or until all the liquid is absorbed.

Dissolve the yeast extract in ¼ pint/140ml warm water. Pour half into a large saucepan and place over a high heat until the liquid bubbles. Add the onion and garlic to this liquid and 'sauté' for 3-5 minutes, stirring frequently until the onions are soft. Add the remaining liquid and the TVP chunks, stir well and leave to cook for 5-10 minutes. Gradually add more water as the TVP chunks soften.

Add the carrots, kidney beans and mushrooms, stir well and add more water according to the consistency you prefer, approximately 1-2 pints/570ml-1 litre. Add the spices, stir well and leave to simmer over a medium heat. Stir occasionally.

When the rice is cooked, gently stir in the chopped fresh parsley. Serve the rice on to two heated plates, make a well in the centre of the rice and fill with the ragoût. Serve immediately.

Grilled Grapefruit
1 large grapefruit, halved
1 tablespoon brown sugar

Pre-heat the grill to a medium setting. Use a serrated knife to prepare the grapefruit halves: cut round the edges and in between the segments. Sprinkle half of the sugar over each grapefruit and place them together on a tray or rack. Place under the hot grill so that there is at least 1 inch/2.5cm between the fruit and the grill element. Cook for 10-15 minutes until the grapefruit is hot all the way through and the sugar topping is slightly caramelized. Serve immediately.

Accompaniments
2 Oat Biscuits per person
Herbal tea

CHINESE MENU

The cookery of China is famous for the variety of dishes served at one meal, each historically packed full of ritual and symbolism. The Chinese developed a cooking technique that did not deplete their scant supplies of fuel so that, generally, Chinese food is very quick to prepare. We have tried to keep the preparation time to these meals to a minimum, while also incorporating many of the staples of Chinese cuisine. In these dishes (as in the Japanese menu), you might try chopping and slicing the fruits and vegetables in a variety of shapes to produce a more authentic-looking dish. These range from tiny cubes to matchstick-sized slices and were originally intended to speed cooking time, while enhancing the nutritional value of each food item.

Breakfast
Fruit Compote
2 Oat Biscuits
Herbal Tea

Snack
3 Oat Biscuits
Mineral Water or Herbal Tea

Lunch
China Rice Salad
2 Oat Biscuits
Herbal Tea or Mineral Water

Snack
3 Oat Biscuits
Mineral Water or Herbal Tea

Dinner
Baked Cabbage Rolls in Mustard Sauce
with
Bean and Mushroom Stir-Fry and Bamboo Shoot and
Broccoli Sauté
2 Oat Biscuits
Herbal Tea

Chinese Shopping List for two people

From your greengrocer:
1 medium onion
1 lb/455g broccoli
6 oz/170g carrots
2 stalks celery
8 oz/225g mushrooms
1 bunch spring onions
1 lb/455g French beans, fresh or frozen
8 cabbage leaves
½ oz/15g fresh parsley
2 oz/55g beansprouts (i.e. alfalfa, mung)
1 lemon (juice of)
2 apples
2 oranges
2 bananas

From your supermarket or health-food shop:
½ pint/285ml Plamil® soya milk concentrate
1 lb/455g tin kidney beans (low-salt variety)
8 oz/225g tin bamboo shoots
10 oz/285g firm tofu
8 oz/225g green peas, tinned or frozen
10 dried prunes
2 oz/55g rolled oats
4 oz/115g rice

And from your own cupboard:
1 tablespoon Marmite yeast extract (or low-salt equivalent)
1 tablespoon prepared mustard
2 tablespoons brewer's yeast
ground or fresh ginger
ground black pepper
ground coriander
ground cinnamon

Chinese Breakfast

Fruit Compote

10 dried prunes, washed
2 apples, cored and chopped
2 oranges, peeled and chopped
2 bananas, sliced
2 oz/55g rolled oats
pinch ground cinnamon

Place the prunes in a deep bowl and cover them with water. If possible, leave them to soak overnight; otherwise, pour boiling water over them in the morning and leave to soak for 20 minutes.

Mix the other fruits together in a large bowl, add the soaked prunes and the prune juice, stir well and spoon into two serving bowls. Mix the oats and cinnamon together and sprinkle half of this mixture over each of the bowls of fruit. Serve immediately.

Accompaniments

2 Oat Biscuits per person
Herbal tea

Chinese Snack

3 Oat Biscuits per person
Mineral water *or* herbal tea

Chinese Lunch

China Rice Salad

4 oz/115g rice
8 oz/225g green peas, tinned or frozen, drained
½ teaspoon freshly ground black pepper
pinch freshly grated or ground ginger
½ teaspoon ground coriander
6 oz/170g carrot, shredded
2 stalks celery, finely chopped
½ oz/15g fresh parsley, chopped
2 oz/55g beansprouts (i.e. alfalfa, mung)
10 oz/285g firm tofu, cubed
2 tablespoons lemon juice

Wash and drain the rice, place in a saucepan and cover with twice its volume of water. Place over a high heat and bring to a boil, stir once, cover the pan and reduce the heat. Leave the rice to simmer undisturbed for 20 minutes, or until the liquid is absorbed. Cook the peas if they are frozen. Stir the peas, pepper, ginger and coriander into the cooked rice and leave the pan uncovered to allow the rice to cool.

Stir in the remaining ingredients when the rice has cooled. Serve immediately or chill for use later.

NOTE: This salad may be prepared the evening before you wish to eat it for lunch.

Accompaniments
2 Oat Biscuits per person
Herbal tea *or* mineral water

Chinese Snack
3 Oat Biscuits per person
Mineral water *or* herbal tea

Chinese Dinner

Baked Cabbage Rolls in Mustard Sauce
8 cabbage leaves
½ tablespoon Marmite yeast extract (or low-salt equivalent)
1 medium onion, peeled and finely chopped
1 lb/455g tin kidney beans, drained
Mustard sauce
½ pint/285ml Plamil® soya milk concentrate
2 tablespoons brewer's yeast
1 tablespoon prepared mustard

Pre-heat the oven to 190°C/375°F (Gas Mark 5). Bring a pot of water to a boil and blanch the cabbage leaves for 2 minutes. Remove them from the water and allow them to drain and cool.

Dissolve the yeast extract in 2 fl oz/60ml warm water. Pour half of this 'gravy' into a frying pan and place over a high heat. When the liquid begins to bubble, add the onion and 'sauté' for 2-3 minutes, until the onion is soft. Add the beans and the remaining gravy and bring this mixture to a simmer, mashing the beans as the mixture cooks.

Measure the Plamil® into a large jug. Add the brewer's yeast and prepared mustard and whisk this sauce to an even consistency.

Place one of the blanched cabbage leaves on the work surface and spoon one-eighth of the bean mixture on to the centre end nearest you. Now roll the cabbage leaf around the mixture and place the roll, seam side down, in a casserole dish. Repeat this process until all eight leaves and all the bean mixture is used. Now pour the mustard sauce over the cabbage rolls, cover the casserole and bake in the hot oven for 30 minutes. Serve hot with the following side dishes.

Bean and Mushroom Stir-Fry

½ tablespoon Marmite yeast extract (or low-salt equivalent)
8 oz/225g mushrooms, sliced
1 lb/455g French beans, fresh or frozen
1 bunch spring onions, trimmed and sliced lengthways

Dissolve the yeast extract in 2 fl oz/60ml warm water. Pour half of this 'gravy' into a frying pan and place over a high heat. When the liquid begins to bubble, add the mushrooms and 'sauté' them for 3-5 minutes, stirring frequently. Add the French beans and the remaining gravy but do not stir them into the mushrooms. Arrange the spring onions on top of the beans, cover the pan and leave it over a low heat for 10-15 minutes. Stir the contents of the pan together just before serving. Serve hot.

Bamboo Shoot and Broccoli Sauté

1 lb/455g broccoli, trimmed and coarsely chopped
8 oz/225g tin bamboo shoots, drained
freshly ground black pepper to taste
freshly grated or ground ginger to taste

Pour 2 fl oz/60ml water into a deep frying pan and place over a high heat until the water begins to bubble. Add the chopped broccoli and the bamboo shoots. Sprinkle the pepper and ginger over the vegetables, cover the pan and leave to cook for 10-15 minutes. Stir the vegetables before serving. Serve hot.

Accompaniments

2 Oat Biscuits per person
Herbal tea

THE GREEK MENU

As you might expect from a Mediterranean country, Greek food is characterized by its abundant use of herbs, lemon and olive oil. Well, we won't be using very much olive oil, but we have included plenty of lemon juice and herbs. Tabbouleh is an excellent example of this combination – a classic Mediterranean dish made with bulgar wheat and fresh (of course!) herbs and vegetables. The Pilaf uses rice in a particularly Greek way, and the Vegetables à la Grecque are just the merest insight into what you can do with vegetables when you let herbs, lemons and a little sun into your cooking.

Breakfast
Fresh Melon
All Bran® Cereal with Plamil® and Dried Fruit
2 Oat Biscuits
Herbal Tea

Snack
3 Oat Biscuits
Mineral Water or Herbal Tea

Lunch
Tabbouleh Salad
Fresh Apple
2 Oat Biscuits
Herbal Tea or Mineral Water

Snack
3 Oat Biscuits
Mineral Water or Herbal Tea

Dinner
Crudités with Tarragon Vinaigrette
Pilaf with Spinach and Chickpea Garnish
and
Vegetables à la Grecque
2 Oat Biscuits
Herbal Tea

Greek Shopping List for two people

From your greengrocer:
8 oz/225g cauliflower
8 oz/225g mushrooms
4 oz/115g carrots
1 lb/455g fresh tomatoes
4 stalks celery
1 medium cucumber
1 lb/455g raw spinach
1 medium onion
1 medium sweet pepper
1 bunch spring onions
3 cloves garlic (optional)
2 sprigs fresh tarragon
1 oz/30g fresh parsley
½ oz/15g fresh mint
4 lemons (juice of)
2 apples
1 melon (honeydew or cantaloupe)

From your supermarket or health-food shop:
All Bran® cereal
2 oz/55g raisins
½ pint/285ml Plamil® soya milk concentrate
8 oz/225g bulgar wheat
6 oz/170g rice
1 sachet/128g Protoveg TVP mince (or equivalent)
6 oz/170g raw chickpeas *or* 2x14 oz/395g tins cooked chickpeas

And from your own cupboard:
ground *or* whole black pepper
ground *or* whole coriander
¼ pint/140ml cider vinegar
dried thyme
bay leaf
1 tablespoon Marmite yeast extract (or low-salt equivalent)

Greek Breakfast

Fresh Melon
Slice one fresh melon in half, remove the seeds and discard. Serve the melon as it is or use a melon scoop to make small balls of melon, leaving them in the melon half.

All Bran® Cereal with Plamil® and Dried Fruit
2 oz/55g All Bran® cereal
½ pint/285ml Plamil® soya milk concentrate
2 oz/55g dried raisins

Measure 1oz/30g of cereal into each of two bowls. Dilute the soya milk with ¼ pint/140ml cold water and stir well. Pour half of this milk over each serving. Sprinkle 1 oz/30g of the raisins over each serving and stir well. Serve immediately.

Accompaniments
2 Oat Biscuits per person
Herbal tea

Greek Snack
3 Oat Biscuits per person
Mineral water *or* herbal tea

Greek Lunch

Tabbouleh Salad
8 oz/225g bulgar wheat
1 medium sweet pepper, de-seeded and chopped
1 bunch spring onions, chopped
1 lb/455g fresh tomatoes, chopped
½ oz/15g fresh parsley, chopped
½ oz/15g fresh mint, chopped
freshly ground black pepper to taste
juice of 3 lemons a little lemon peel, grated

Measure the bulgar into a pan or bowl and slowly pour 16 fl oz/455ml boiling water over. Stir once then leave to one side while you prepare the vegetables.

Add the sweet pepper, onions, tomatoes, fresh herbs and black pepper and gently fold these ingredients into the bulgar. Pour the lemon juice over all and sprinkle a little grated lemon rind over the top. Chill the salad then stir again and serve.

Accompaniments
1 fresh apple per person
2 Oat Biscuits per person
Herbal tea *or* mineral water

Greek Snack
3 Oat Biscuits per person
Mineral water *or* herbal tea

Greek Dinner

Crudités with Tarragon Vinaigrette
4 oz/115g carrots, cut into sticks
4 stalks celery, cut into sticks
1 medium cucumber, cut into chunks
Tarragon vinaigrette
¼ pint/140ml cider vinegar
2 or more sprigs fresh tarragon, finely chopped
freshly ground black pepper to taste

Prepare the vegetables and place them upright in a small, deep bowl. Measure the vinegar into a bowl and stir in the tarragon and pepper. Pour the vinaigrette over the crudités and serve.

Pilaf
6 oz/170g rice
1 sachet/128g Protoveg TVP mince (or equivalent)
1 tablespoon Marmite yeast extract (or low-salt equivalent)
1 medium onion, peeled and finely chopped
½ teaspoon freshly ground black pepper
½ teaspoon dried thyme

Wash and drain the rice and place it in a large saucepan. Add the TVP to the rice and stir well. Now pour 1½ pints/850ml water over this mixture and place over a high heat. Bring to a boil, cover the pan and reduce the heat.

Dissolve the yeast extract in ¼ pint/140ml warm water. Pour a little of this 'gravy' into a frying pan and place over a high heat. When the liquid bubbles, add the chopped onion and 'sauté' for 2-3 minutes, stirring frequently. When the onions are tender, add the pepper, thyme and remaining 'gravy' and stir well. Add this sauté to the cooking rice and TVP mixture, stir once, re-cover the pan and leave to simmer for a further 20 minutes, until all the liquid is absorbed.

Press the rice mixture into a ring mould and cover with the plate it will be turned on to. Wrap in a towel until ready to serve to keep it hot. When the garnish is ready, turn the rice out on to the plate and fill the centre of the ring with the garnish. Serve immediately.

Spinach and Chickpea Garnish

6 oz/170g raw chickpeas *or* 2x14 oz/395g tins cooked chickpeas, drained
3 cloves garlic, finely chopped (optional)
1 lb/455g raw spinach, washed, trimmed and thinly sliced

If using raw chickpeas, cook them in a pressure cooker. Turn the chickpeas into a large frying pan or saucepan and place over a high heat. Add a little water if necessary to prevent scorching, but avoid all but the minimum amount of liquid. Add the garlic to the chickpeas (garlic really does enhance this dish!) and stir well.

Pack the spinach into the pan and cover firmly. Leave over the high heat for 5 minutes, undisturbed. Then reduce the heat and stir the mixture well. Cover the pan again and leave cooking for a further 5-10 minutes, until the spinach is tender.

Vegetables à la Grecque

8 oz/225g cauliflower, coarsely chopped
8 oz/225g mushrooms, sliced
½ oz/15g fresh parsley, finely chopped
½ teaspoon ground coriander *or* crushed coriander seeds
freshly ground black pepper to taste
juice of 1 lemon (or more if desired)

Pour 2 fl oz/60ml water into a large pan and place over a high heat. When the water is bubbling, add the cauliflower and mushrooms and stir frequently as they cook, about 5 minutes. The vegetables may brown slightly. Add a tiny amount of water if necessary, then sprinkle the parsley, coriander and pepper over the mixture and stir well. Cover the pan and reduce the heat to a low or medium temperature. Leave to cook for a further 5 minutes. Turn into a hot serving dish, pour the lemon juice over and serve immediately.

Accompaniments
2 Oat Biscuits per person
Herbal tea

THE INDIAN MENU

Hopefully, you are not a victim of too much over-exaggerated Indian cooking, where the spices are far too hot, poorly blended and each dish is buried beneath a layer of orange oil. Authentic, carefully prepared Indian cooking is nothing like that. It includes strong spices certainly, but it also uses some exceptionally subtle blends of herb, spice and flavour to achieve the colourful and aromatic dishes for which it is famous. We have tried here to offer you a very small flavour of Indian cooking – without the oil. The Spicy Vinaigrette for example, is rather like an Indian pickle with plenty of scope for you to manipulate its flavour by adding or altering spices. Try other spices – such as cardamom, garlic and fenugreek – when you cook it.

Breakfast
Fruity Muesli
2 Oat Biscuits
Herbal Tea

Snack
3 Oat Biscuits
Mineral Water or Herbal Tea

Lunch
Spicy Vinaigrette Salad
2 Oat Biscuits
Herbal Tea or Mineral Water

Snack
3 Oat Biscuits
Mineral Water or Herbal Tea

Dinner
Dhal Soup
Biriani Rice with Sag Aloo and Bean and Mushroom Curry
2 Oat Biscuits
Herbal Tea

Indian Shopping List for two people

From your greengrocer:
1 lb/455g cauliflower
8 oz/225g potatoes
8 oz/225g cabbage
4 oz/115g carrots
1 medium onion
1 medium turnip
3 cloves garlic (optional)
1 medium sweet pepper
1 bunch spring onions
8 oz/225g mushrooms
1 lb/455g fresh spinach
2 tomatoes
1 oz/30g fresh coriander leaves
1 banana
1 lemon
2 apples

From your supermarket or health-food shop:
10 dried dates
2oz/55g rolled oats
2 tablespoons oat bran
½ pint/285ml Plamil® soya milk concentrate
4 oz/115g raisins
8 oz/225g raw red lentils
8 oz/225g rice
1 sachet /128g Protoveg TVP chunks or mince (or equivalent)
1 lb/455g tin kidney beans (low-salt variety)

And from your own cupboard:
1 tablespoon Marmite yeast extract (or low-salt equivalent)
¼ pint /140ml cider vinegar
2 tablespoons brewer's yeast
1½ teaspoons ground cumin
1½ teaspoons chilli powder
ground *or* whole black pepper
ground *or* whole cloves
fresh *or* ground ginger
ground nutmeg

Indian Breakfast

Fruity Muesli
2 oz/55g rolled oats
2 tablespoons oat bran
4 oz/115g raisins
2 apples, cored and chopped
1 banana, sliced
10 dried dates, washed and chopped
½ pint /285ml Plamil® soya milk concentrate

Mix the first six ingredients together in a large bowl. Divide the mixture into two portions and spoon into separate serving bowls. Dilute the soya milk with ¼ pint/140ml cold water and pour half of this milk over each serving. Stir and serve.

Accompaniments
2 Oat Biscuits per person
Herbal tea

Indian Snack
3 Oat Biscuits per person
Mineral water *or* herbal tea

Indian Lunch

Spicy Vinaigrette Salad
1 lb/455g cauliflower, chopped
4 oz/115g carrots, thinly sliced
1 medium turnip, peeled and shredded
8 oz/225g cabbage, shredded
1 medium sweet pepper, de-seeded and chopped
Spicy Vinaigrette
¼ pint/140ml cider vinegar
½ teaspoon ground black pepper *or* 12 whole peppercorns
¼ teaspoon ground cloves *or* 6 whole cloves
ground *or* freshly grated ginger to taste

Place the vegetables in a deep enamel saucepan and pour the vinaigrette over. Stir well, cover the pan and place over a medium heat. Leave to cook, undisturbed, for 15-20 minutes. Remove from the heat and allow to cool. Chill and serve.

Accompaniments
2 Oat Biscuits per person
Herbal tea *or* mineral water

Indian Snack
3 Oat Biscuits per person
Mineral water *or* herbal tea

Indian Dinner

Dhal Soup
8 oz/225g raw red lentils
1 tablespoon Marmite yeast extract (or low-salt equivalent)
1 medium onion, peeled and chopped
½ teaspoon ground or crushed cumin
¼-½ teaspoon chilli powder
½ oz/15g fresh coriander leaves, finely chopped

Wash and drain the lentils, place in a deep saucepan and cover
with twice their volume of water. Place over a high heat and bring
to a boil. Reduce the heat, cover the pan and leave to simmer for 20
minutes.

Dissolve the yeast extract in 2 fl oz/60ml warm water and pour
into a frying pan. Place over a high heat until the liquid begins to
bubble. Add the onion and 'sauté' for 2-3 minutes, until the onion
softens. Add the cumin and chilli powder and stir frequently for a
further 2 minutes. Remove from the heat and add this sauté to the
cooking lentils.

When the lentils are soft and mushy, add the coriander leaves,
stir well and serve immediately.

Biriani Rice
8 oz/225g rice
1 sachet /128g Protoveg TVP mince or chunks (or equivalent)
½ oz/15g fresh coriander leaves, finely chopped
¼ teaspoon ground nutmeg
juice of 1 lemon

Wash and drain the rice, place in a deep saucepan and cover with
twice its volume of water. Place over a high heat and bring to a boil,
then reduce the heat, cover the pan and leave to simmer until the
liquid is absorbed, about 20 minutes.

Place the TVP in a separate pan and cover with twice its volume
of water. Place over a high heat until the water begins to boil, then
reduce the heat and simmer for 10-15 minutes, until the TVP is
tender. Drain any excess liquid off.

Turn the rice and TVP into a large serving bowl, add the
coriander leaves, nutmeg and lemon juice and gently turn them
together. Serve immediately with the following side dishes.

Sag Aloo

8 oz/225g potatoes, peeled and cubed
1 tablespoon brewer's yeast
½ teaspoon ground cumin
¼ teaspoon chilli powder
3 cloves garlic, finely chopped
1 lb/455g fresh spinach, washed, trimmed and thinly sliced
2 whole tomatoes, chopped

Place the potato cubes into a steamer, cover the pan and steam until they are just tender. Remove from the heat.

Stir the yeast, cumin and chilli powder into 2 fl oz/60ml water and pour into a deep pan. Place over a high heat until the liquid begins to bubble, then add the garlic. Stir frequently while the garlic softens.

Add the steamed potatoes and the spinach to the sauté, cover the pan and leave to cook over a medium heat for 10-15 minutes, until the potatoes and spinach are well cooked. Add the chopped tomatoes and continue to cook for 5 minutes, stirring frequently. Serve immediately.

Bean and Mushroom Curry

1 lb/455g tin kidney beans
8 oz/225g mushrooms, sliced
1 tablespoon brewer's yeast
1 bunch spring onions, trimmed and chopped
½ teaspoon ground or crushed cumin
¼-½ teaspoon chilli powder

Pour the beans into a large frying pan and place over a high heat. Add the mushrooms and yeast, stir well and cook for 5 minutes. Reduce the heat, add the onions and spices and stir well. Cover and cook over a low heat for 10-15 minutes. Serve hot.

Accompaniments
2 Oat Biscuits per person
Herbal tea

THE ITALIAN MENU

Not just a bowl of pasta! Italian cookery has evolved from the ancient Greek, Roman and Oriental worlds. The quality of Italian food derives from its ability to take the most basic foods and the simplest recipes and *perfect* them. What could be more basic than a flour and water paste? Or a bowl of beans, dressed in herbs and vinegar? Even the humble tomato becomes a masterpiece sauce in the hands of a good Italian cook. Here, we give you the outline – you add the love and fuss and perfection that can only be added at the moment when the flavours merge.

Breakfast
Refreshing Fruit Bowl
2 Oat Biscuits
Herbal Tea

Snack
3 Oat Biscuits
Herbal Tea or Mineral Water

Lunch
Fagioli Salad
2 Oat Biscuits
Herbal Tea or Mineral Water

Snack
3 Oat Biscuits
Herbal Tea or Mineral Water

Dinner
Bolognaise Soup
Pasta con Funghi with Insalata Tricolore
2 Oat Biscuits
Herbal Tea

Italian Shopping List for two people

From your greengrocer:
2 medium onions
2 medium turnips
6 oz/170g red cabbage
8 oz/225g mushrooms
4 oz/115g broccoli
4 tomatoes
1 small Cos lettuce
3 cloves garlic (optional)
1 oz/30g fresh parsley
2 oranges
1 grapefruit
2 bananas

From your supermarket or health-food shop:
2x14 oz/395g tins chopped tomatoes
1 sachet /128g Protoveg TVP mince or equivalent (optional)
8 oz/225g tinned or frozen sweetcorn
½ pint /285ml Plamil® soya milk concentrate
1 lb/455g tin white beans (i.e. haricot, butter)
11 fl oz/315ml cider vinegar
8 oz/225g eggless spaghetti or other pasta
10 dried prunes
2 tablespoons rolled oats

And from your own cupboard:
1 tablespoon Marmite yeast extract (or low-salt equivalent)
1 teaspoon prepared mustard
ground cinnamon
ground black pepper
dried basil
dried oregano
bay leaf

Italian Breakfast

Refreshing Fruit Bowl
10 dried prunes, washed
2 oranges, peeled and chopped
1 grapefruit, peeled and chopped
2 bananas, sliced
2 tablespoons rolled oats
pinch ground cinnamon

Soak the prunes in cold water overnight, or pour boiling water over them in the morning and leave to soak for 20 minutes. Mix all the fruit together in a large bowl and pour the prune juice over. Stir well then spoon into two serving bowls. Mix the oats and cinnamon together and sprinkle half over each of the two servings. Serve immediately.

Accompaniments
2 Oat Biscuits per person
Herbal Tea

Italian Snack
3 Oat Biscuits per person
Herbal tea *or* mineral water

Italian Lunch

Fagioli Salad
½ pint/285 ml cider vinegar
6 oz/170g red cabbage, shredded
freshly ground black pepper to taste
1 lb/455g tin white beans (i.e. haricot, butter), drained
1 oz/30g fresh parsley, chopped

Measure the vinegar into an enamel saucepan, place over a medium heat and bring to a simmer. Add the cabbage, black pepper and beans and stir well. Cover the pan and leave to simmer for 5 minutes, then remove from the heat and add the parsley. Stir well and serve hot or cold.
NOTE: This salad may be made the evening before you wish to serve it at lunch and kept chilled in the refrigerator.

Accompaniments
2 Oat Biscuits per person
Herbal tea *or* mineral water

Italian Snack
3 Oat Biscuits per person
Herbal tea *or* mineral water

Italian Dinner

Bolognaise Soup

1 tablespoon Marmite yeast extract (or low-salt equivalent)
1 medium onion, peeled and chopped
1 clove garlic, chopped (optional)
1 sachet /128g Protoveg TVP mince or equivalent (optional)
2x14 oz/395g tins chopped tomatoes
4 oz /115g broccoli, chopped
8 oz/225g tinned or frozen sweetcorn
½ teaspoon dried basil
½ teaspoon dried oregano
freshly ground black pepper to taste
2 bay leaves

Dissolve the yeast extract in ½ pint/285ml warm water and pour 2-3 tablespoons of this liquid into a deep saucepan. Place the pan over a medium heat and add the onion and garlic. Stir frequently to 'sauté' the onion until tender. If using TVP, add it now with an additional ½ pint/285ml water, and stir well. Gradually add the remaining yeast liquid and leave the mixture to simmer gently for 5 minutes.

Add the remaining ingredients to the saucepan, stir well and leave to simmer gently for 15-20 minutes. Add more water if desired. Serve this soup hot or cold in a brightly coloured bowl.

Pasta con Funghi

1 medium onion, peeled and finely chopped
2 cloves garlic, chopped (optional)
8 oz/225g mushrooms, sliced
freshly ground black pepper to taste
8 oz/225g raw, eggless spaghetti or other pasta
8 fl oz/225ml Plamil® soya milk concentrate

Pour 2 fl oz/60ml water into a deep frying pan and place over a high heat. When the water bubbles, add the onion and garlic and stir frequently while they soften. Add the mushrooms and pepper, stir well and cover the pan. Leave to simmer gently over a low heat while you prepare the pasta.

Bring a large pot of water to a boil and add the pasta to it. Stir occasionally and leave the pasta to boil for about 12 minutes, until just tender. Add the soya milk to the mushroom mixture and leave over a medium heat to bring it to a slow simmer, stirring often. Drain the pasta and pour the mushroom sauce over it. Stir well and serve on heated plates.

Insalata Tricolore
2 medium turnips, peeled and cooked *or* shredded raw
2 fl oz/60ml Plamil® soya milk concentrate
freshly ground black pepper to taste
4 Cos lettuce leaves, thinly sliced
4 tomatoes, sliced
Dressing
1 fl oz/30ml cider vinegar
1 teaspoon prepared mustard
pinch dried basil

Turnip may be eaten raw or cooked, so you may decide which you prefer today. If eating it raw, simply shred it, sprinkle with a little pepper and add the soya milk to the dressing ingredients. If eating it cooked, cut the turnip into cubes and steam them until tender. Then mash the turnip in a bowl with the soya milk to make a purée. Add black pepper to taste.

Arrange the lettuce, tomato and turnip in three distinct wedges or lines on each of two plates (Insalata Tricolore means three-colour salad). Place the dressing ingredients in a jug or jar, including the soya milk if using raw turnip, and stir or shake until smooth. Pour over the salad and serve.

Accompaniments
2 Oat Biscuits per person
Herbal tea

THE JAPANESE MENU

Japanese food is characterized by its simplicity and lightness. Like Chinese cooking, Japanese meals are presented in small portions of several different dishes. Of course, we haven't included the famous Tempura, which is fried, nor the sea foods and highly salted foods such as Miso and soy sauce. Instead, we have relied on the historical preference for dishes that are delicate in flavour, texture and appearance to create meals that fulfill, without overwhelming, your taste buds! Prepare this menu when you are really hungry – the meals are surprisingly filling.

Breakfast
Spicy Apple Porridge
2 Oat Biscuits
Herbal Tea

Snack
3 Oat Biscuits
Herbal Tea or Mineral Water

Lunch
Vegetable Soup
Five Vegetable Salad
2 Oat Biscuits
Herbal Tea 2or Mineral Water

Snack
3 Oat Biscuits
Herbal Tea or Mineral Water

Dinner
Mushroom and Cabbage Stir-Fry
with
Sautéed Broccoli and Brussels Sprouts
over
Steamed Rice and Beans with Carrot and Ginger Marinade
2 Oat Biscuits
Herbal Tea

Japanese Shopping List for two people

From your greengrocer:
1 lb/455g cabbage
12 oz/340g carrots
2 medium turnips
1 medium onion
8 oz/225g broccoli
8 oz/225g Brussels sprouts
8 oz/225g mushrooms
1 medium sweet pepper
1 bunch spring onions
1 oz/30g fresh parsley
1 oz/30g fresh ginger
2 apples

From your supermarket or health-food shop:
½ pint/285ml Plamil® soya milk concentrate
4 oz/115g rolled oats
1 lb/455g French beans, tinned, frozen or fresh
½ pint/285ml cider vinegar
10 oz/285g soft or firm tofu
8 oz/225g rice
1 lb/455g tin kidney beans

And from your own cupboard:
1 tablespoon Marmite yeast extract (or low-salt equivalent)
2 tablespoons brewer's yeast
ground cinnamon *or* allspice
ground black pepper

Japanese Breakfast

Spicy Apple Porridge
   4 oz/115g rolled *or* porridge oats
   ½ teaspoon ground cinnamon *or* allspice
   ½ pint/285ml Plamil® soya milk concentrate
   2 apples, cored and finely chopped
   Mix the oats and spice together in a deep saucepan. Dilute the
soya milk with ½ pint/285ml water and pour over the oat mixture.
Place over a medium heat and stir constantly while the porridge
thickens. Add the apples 2-3 minutes before serving the porridge.
Divide into two portions.
NOTE: If you prefer a cold breakfast, simply mix these ingredients, diluting the soya milk to taste.

Accompaniments
2 Oat Biscuits per person
Herbal tea

Japanese Snack
3 Oat Biscuits per person
Herbal tea *or* mineral water

Japanese Lunch

Vegetable Soup
　　4 oz/115g cabbage, shredded
　　4 oz/115g carrots, sliced
　　4 oz/115g turnip, peeled and chopped
　　1 bunch spring onions, chopped
　　8oz/225g French beans
　　½ tablespoon Marmite yeast extract (or low-salt equivalent)
　　freshly ground black pepper to taste
　　1 oz/30g fresh parsley, chopped

Measure the first five ingredients into a large saucepan and
cover with water. Place over a high heat and bring the liquid to a
boil. Reduce the heat and stir in the yeast extract and black pepper.
Cover the pan and simmer for 15 minutes. Stir in the fresh parsley
and simmer, uncovered, for a further 5 minutes then serve.
NOTE: If you prefer, you may enjoy this soup at dinner instead of,
or as well as, at lunch.

Five Vegetable Salad
　　4 oz/115g cabbage, shredded
　　4 oz/115g carrots, shredded
　　4 oz/115g turnip, peeled and shredded
　　1 medium sweet pepper, de-seeded and sliced
　　8 oz/225g French beans
　　Dressing
　　¼ pint/140ml cider vinegar
　　1 tablespoon brewer's yeast
　　freshly ground black pepper to taste

Place the vegetables in a large salad bowl. Mix the dressing ingredients together in a jar or jug and pour over the salad. Toss the
salad and serve.

Accompaniments
2 Oat Biscuits per person
Herbal tea *or* mineral water

Japanese Snack
3 Oat Biscuits per person
Herbal tea *or* mineral water

Japanese Dinner

Mushroom and Cabbage Stir-Fry
  1 medium onion, peeled and chopped
  8 oz/225g mushrooms, sliced
  8 oz/225g cabbage, shredded
  freshly ground black pepper to taste
  pinch ground allspice *or* cinnamon

Pour 2 fl oz/60ml water into a large frying pan and place over a high heat. When the water bubbles, add the onion and stir frequently while it softens. Add the mushrooms and cabbage and do not stir. Instead, sprinkle the pepper and spice over the cabbage, cover the pan and leave over a medium to low heat for 15 minutes. Stir the contents well and cook, uncovered, for a further 5 minutes. Serve hot.

Sautéed Broccoli and Brussels Sprouts
  ½ tablespoon Marmite yeast extract (or low-salt equivalent)
  8 oz/225g broccoli, trimmed and chopped
  8 oz/225g Brussels sprouts, halved

Dissolve the yeast extract in 2 fl oz/60ml warm water and pour into a saucepan. Place over a high heat. When the liquid begins to bubble, add the vegetables and stir constantly for 1-2 minutes. Then cover the pan, reduce the heat and leave to cook for 5 minutes. Stir the contents again, cover the pan and cook for a final 2-3 minutes. Serve hot.

Steamed Rice and Beans
  8 oz/225g rice
  1 lb/455g tin kidney beans, drained
  freshly ground black pepper to taste

Wash and drain the rice, place in a deep saucepan and cover with twice its volume in water. Place over a high heat until the liquid begins to boil, then reduce the heat, cover the pan and leave to simmer for 25 minutes, until the liquid is absorbed.

Heat the beans in a separate saucepan, adding a little black pepper when they are warmed through. Serve the rice on warm plates and spoon the beans over each serving.

Carrot and Ginger Marinade
¼ pint/140ml cider vinegar
1 tablespoon brewer's yeast
½ teaspoon fresh root ginger, grated
10 oz/285g firm or soft tofu, cubed
4 oz/115g carrot, shredded

Mix the vinegar, yeast and ginger together in a jug. Arrange the tofu cubes and shredded carrot in a bowl or casserole dish and pour the marinade over. Leave to sit for as long as possible before the meal – all day if you can, but at least 20 minutes. Serve as a side dish to the others in this meal by lifting the tofu and carrots out of the marinade. If you prefer a hot dish, turn the whole marinade into a saucepan and warm through.

Accompaniments
2 Oat Biscuits per person
Herbal tea

THE MEXICAN MENU

This cuisine is an amalgam of Aztec, Spanish and Central American Indian influences which have produced a cooking famous for chilli peppers, tortillas (pancakes made from maize) and beans. Rice and a whole variety of grains and tubers are also staples but, in foreign terms, they are not so strongly associated with Mexican food. Also not well known is that Mexico grows a huge variety of fresh fruit – so we have included a fruit-only lunch just to give you the experience! Frying was a fairly late introduction to Mexico so we have, naturally, left it out of these meals. Instead, we suggest you enjoy the spicy flavours set against very basic foods, even doubling up on the amounts of chilli powder listed here. You never know, you might want to enter the Chilli Eating Contest held every year on the border between Mexico and Texas!

Breakfast
All Bran® Cereal with Plamil® and Dried Fruit
Fresh Grapefruit
2 Oat Biscuits
Herbal Tea

Snack
3 Oat Biscuits
Herbal Tea or Mineral Water

Lunch
Fresh Fruit Platter
2 Oat Biscuits
Herbal Tea or Mineral Water

Snack
3 Oat Biscuits
Herbal Tea or Mineral Water

Dinner
Chilli Beans
Tostadas with Salad Selection and Tangy Sauce
2 Oat Biscuits
Herbal Tea

Mexican Shopping List for two people

From your greengrocer:
1 medium onion
2 medium carrots
4 oz/115g mushrooms
1 head loose-leaf lettuce
1 medium sweet pepper
1 oz/30g fresh parsley
2 oranges
1 grapefruit
4 oz/115g grapes
1 small melon (honeydew or cantaloupe)
2 bananas
2 apples

From your supermarket or health-food shop:
½ pint/285ml Plamil® soya milk concentrate
All Bran® cereal
2 oz/55g raisins
1 sachet/128g Protoveg TVP mince (or equivalent)
14 oz/395g tin chopped tomatoes
1 lb/455g tin kidney beans
12 oz/340g tin sweetcorn
8 tostadas (corn meal pancakes)
8 oz/225g raw red lentils
4 oz/115g tin tomato purée

And from your own cupboard:
1 tablespoon Marmite yeast extract (or low-salt equivalent)
1 tablespoon brewer's yeast
1 teaspoon molasses
2 tablespoons cider vinegar
dried basil
chilli powder
bay leaf

Mexican Breakfast

All Bran® Cereal with Plamil® and Dried Fruit
    2 oz/55g All Bran® cereal
    2 oz/55g dried raisins
    ½ pint/285ml Plamil® soya milk concentrate

Mix the cereal and raisins together. Dilute the milk with ¼ pint/140ml cold water, stir and pour over each serving.

Fresh Grapefruit

Slice one large grapefruit in half, then use a serrated knife to cut round the edges and segments. Serve half to each person. Alternatively, peel the grapefruit, divide it into segments and chop these in half. Serve half to each person.

Accompaniments
2 Oat Biscuits per person
Herbal tea

Mexican Snack
3 Oat Biscuits per person
Herbal tea *or* mineral water

Mexican Lunch

Fresh Fruit Platter
2 oranges, peeled and divided into segments
2 large slices melon (honeydew or cantaloupe)
4 oz/115g grapes, washed
2 bananas, sliced
2 apples, quartered

Prepare the fruit and arrange them together on a brightly coloured plate. The more creativity you put into this arrangement, the more you will enjoy this meal!

Accompaniments
2 Oat Biscuits per person
Herbal tea *or* mineral water

Mexican Snack
3 Oat Biscuits per person
Herbal tea *or* mineral water

Mexican Dinner

Chilli Beans
½ tablespoon Marmite yeast extract (or low-salt equivalent)
1 medium onion, peeled and chopped
½ sachet/64g Protoveg TVP mince (or equivalent)
¼-½ teaspoon chilli powder
14oz/395g tin chopped tomatoes
1 lb/455g tin kidney beans, drained
12 oz/340g tin sweetcorn, drained
2 bay leaves

Dissolve the yeast extract in ¼ pint/140ml warm water. Pour half of this into a large saucepan and place over a high heat. When the liquid begins to bubble, add the chopped onion and 'sauté' for 2-3 minutes, until the onion is tender. Add the TVP and the remaining liquid, reduce the heat to a medium setting and leave to cook for another 2-3 minutes, stirring occasionally. Sprinkle the chilli powder over this mixture and stir well.

Add the remaining ingredients, stir them together and add more water if necessary to achieve a thick soup consistency. Cover the pan, leave over a medium heat for 15-20 minutes, stirring occasionally. Serve hot in deep bowls.

Tostadas with Salad Selection and Tangy Sauce

8 tostadas (corn meal pancakes)
½ tablespoon Marmite yeast extract (or low-salt equivalent)
½ sachet/64g Protoveg TVP mince (or equivalent)
8 oz/225g raw red lentils, washed and drained
freshly ground black pepper to taste

Salad Selection	Tangy Sauce
1 head lettuce, thinly sliced	4 oz/115g tin tomato purée
2 medium carrots, shredded	1 tablespoon brewer's yeast
4 oz/115g mushrooms, sliced	1 teaspoon molasses
1 pepper, thinly sliced	2 tablespoons cider vinegar
1 oz/30g fresh parsley, chopped	¼-½ teaspoon chilli powder
lemon juice (optional)	

Pre-heat the oven to 170°C/325°F (Gas Mark 3) and arrange the tostadas on a tray. Dissolve the yeast extract in 1 pint/570ml warm water. Measure the TVP and red lentils into a saucepan, pour the liquid over and place over a high heat. Bring the liquid to a boil, reduce heat, cover pan and simmer for 15-20 minutes, stirring occasionally. Add more water if necessary to make a thick paste.

Prepare each vegetable and place in a separate bowl or plate. Pour a little lemon juice over each prepared vegetable if you wish. Place the tostadas in the hot oven and bake for 3-5 minutes.

Mix all the sauce ingredients together in a small saucepan and stir well. Place over a low heat and bring to a simmer, stirring.

Place two cooked tostadas on each plate and spread a thick layer of the lentil and TVP paste over them. Now arrange a little of each salad vegetable over the paste and finally, spoon a little of the hot sauce over that. Serve at once and come back for a second helping!

Accompaniments
2 Oat Biscuits per person
Herbal tea

THE NEW YORK DELI MENU

'Delis' are delicatessens which, in New York, are present on just about every street. How else can a person get a sandwich and salad at any time of day or night? The cooks behind the counter of most New York delis understand a person's need to, just occasionally, have food like Mom used to make, and they do their best to lavish the love along with the ever-present mayonnaise. We have left out that mayonnaise, but offer you a new and much healthier alternative. We suggest this menu for those days when what you really want is to feel that nothing whatsoever has changed. We don't think you'll notice what has.

Breakfast
All Bran® Cereal with Plamil®
Orange Juice
2 Oat Biscuits
Herbal Tea

Snack
3 Oat Biscuits
Herbal Tea or Mineral Water

Lunch
Waldorf Salad with Special Mayonnaise
Club Sandwich
2 Oat Biscuits
Herbal Tea or Mineral Water

Snack
3 Oat Biscuits
Herbal Tea or Mineral Water

Dinner
Meatloaf with Gravy and Three Veg
2 Oat Biscuits
Herbal Tea

New York Deli Shopping List for two people

From your greengrocer:
1 lb/455g potatoes
1 lb/455g Brussels sprouts
8 oz/225g cabbage
1 medium onion
8 lettuce leaves
4 medium tomatoes
4 stalks celery
fresh parsley, mint or thyme
2 apples
2 bananas
1 lemon (juice of)

From your supermarket or health-food shop:
2 oz/55g All Bran® cereal
¾ pint/340ml Plamil® soya milk concentrate
1 pint/570ml orange juice
12 oz/340g tin sweetcorn
8 slices bread
10 oz/285g firm tofu
2 oz/55g raw red lentils
1 oz/30g rolled oats
1 sachet/128g Protoveg TVP mince (or equivalent)
2 tablespoons tomato purée

And from your own cupboard:
1 tablespoon Marmite yeast extract (or low-salt equivalent)
2 tablespoons brewer's yeast
3 teaspoons prepared mustard
1 teaspoon caraway seeds
ground black pepper
2 teaspoons mixed sweet herbs
bay leaf

New York Deli Breakfast

All Bran® Cereal with Plamil®
2 oz/55g All Bran® cereal
½ pint/285 ml Plamil® soya milk concentrate

Divide the cereal between two bowls. Dilute the soya milk with ¼ pint/140ml cold water, whisk and pour over the cereal. Serve at once.

Accompaniments
½ pint/285ml fresh orange juice per person
2 Oat Biscuits per person
Herbal tea

New York Deli Snack
3 Oat Biscuits per person
Herbal tea *or* mineral water

New York Deli Lunch

Waldorf Salad with Special Mayonnaise
    2 apples, cored and finely chopped
    2 bananas, thinly sliced
    4 stalks celery, finely chopped
    12 oz/340g tin sweetcorn, drained
    Mayonnaise
    2 fl oz/60ml Plamil® soya milk concentrate
    1 tablespoon lemon juice
    1 teaspoon prepared mustard

Mix the fruit and vegetables together in a large bowl. Measure the mayonnaise ingredients together into a jug or jar and stir or shake them well. Pour over the vegetables and toss the salad well. Serve chilled if possible.

Club Sandwich
    8 slices bread
    2 teaspoons prepared mustard
    8 lettuce leaves, washed
    4 medium tomatoes, sliced
    10 oz/285g firm tofu, sliced into strips

Arrange the slices of bread in pairs and spread a little mustard on one slice from each set. Place two lettuce leaves on the other slice of bread in each pair. Arrange the sliced tomato on top of the lettuce, then the tofu strips over the tomato. Finally, close each sandwich with the mustard-coated bread slices and serve.

Accompaniments
2 Oat Biscuits per person
Herbal tea *or* mineral water

New York Deli Snack
3 Oat Biscuits per person
Herbal tea *or* mineral water

New York Deli Dinner

Meatloaf with Gravy and Three Veg

   1 sachet/128g Protoveg TVP mince (or equivalent)
   2 oz/55g raw red lentils, washed and drained
   1 oz/30g rolled oats
   ½ teaspoon freshly ground black pepper
   1½ teaspoons mixed sweet dry herbs
   2 tablespoons tomato purée

Pre-heat the oven to 190°C/375°F (Gas Mark 5) and lightly oil a 1 lb/455g loaf tin. Mix the first five ingredients together. Dissolve tomato purée in 1¼ pints/710ml warm water and pour over dry mixture. Stir well; leave for 5 minutes. Stir again, press into the loaf tin, cover with baking foil and bake for 45 minutes. Serve hot.

Gravy

   1 tablespoon Marmite yeast extract (or low-salt equivalent)
   1 medium onion, peeled and finely chopped
   2 tablespoons brewer's yeast
   ½ teaspoon mixed sweet dry herbs
   freshly ground black pepper to taste
   1 bay leaf

Dissolve yeast extract in ½ pint/285ml warm water. Pour a little into a saucepan and place over high heat. When the liquid bubbles, add the onion and 'sauté' for 2-3 minutes, stirring. Reduce heat and sprinkle yeast, herbs and pepper over the onion. Stir constantly and add the remaining liquid. Add bay leaf, reduce heat to low and leave to simmer.

Three Veg

   1 lb/455g potatoes, scrubbed and quartered
   1 lb/455g Brussels sprouts, trimmed and 'crossed'
   fresh parsley, mint or thyme
   8 oz/225g cabbage, shredded
   1 teaspoon caraway seed

Steam potatoes and Brussels sprouts until tender. Turn into warmed dishes, garnish with herbs and serve. Pour 2 fl oz/60ml water into a large frying pan and place over a high heat. When the liquid bubbles, add cabbage and caraway seed. Cover pan and reduce heat. Cook for 15-20 minutes. Stir together and serve hot.

Accompaniments
2 Oat Biscuits per person
Herbal tea

THE TRADITIONAL ENGLISH MENU

We couldn't decide how far back in English history we should go to fulfill tradition. So we agreed to span the ages and select the most mouthwatering meals from olden times, which still grace English tables. The Great English Fry-Up for breakfast (without the fry), the Ever So Posh Cucumber Sandwiches for lunch (with a lot more as well), and the Working Man's Tea for dinner (with very little work and loved by men and women alike). We had fun creating this menu and went to bed feeling well fed and rosy-cheeked.

Breakfast
Grilled Tomatoes and Mushrooms with Toast and Baked Beans
Fresh Orange
2 Oat Biscuits
Herbal Tea

Snack
3 Oat Biscuits
Herbal Tea or Mineral Water

Lunch
Salad Sandwiches
2 Oat Biscuits
Herbal Tea or Mineral Water

Snack
3 Oat Biscuits
Herbal Tea or Mineral Water

Dinner
Pea Soup
Shepherd's Pie with Green Vegetables
Banana Shake
2 Oat Biscuits
Herbal Tea

Traditional English Shopping List for two people

From your greengrocer:
8 oz/225g potatoes
8 oz/225g Brussels sprouts
8 oz/225g French beans
2 medium onions
4 oz/115g carrots
1 medium cucumber

4 medium tomatoes
4 oz/115g mushrooms
2 cloves garlic (optional)
8 lettuce leaves
2 oranges
2 bananas

From your supermarket or health-food shop:
8 oz/225g raw split green peas
10 slices bread
1 lb/455g tin baked beans in tomato sauce
12 fl oz/340ml Plamil® soya milk concentrate
6 oz/170g tin sweetcorn
1 sachet/128g Protoveg TVP mince *or* chunks (or equivalent)

And from your own cupboard:
1 tablespoon Marmite yeast extract (or low-salt equivalent)
2 tablespoons brewer's yeast
2 teaspoons prepared mustard
½ teaspoon dried thyme
½ teaspoon dried oregano
ground black pepper
ground nutmeg
ground coriander

Traditional English Breakfast

Grilled Tomatoes and Mushrooms with Toast and Baked Beans
1 lb/455g tin baked beans in tomato sauce
4 medium tomatoes, halved
4 oz/115g mushrooms, cleaned
2 slices bread

Pour the baked beans into a small saucepan and place over a medium heat. Stir frequently while the beans heat through. Arrange the tomatoes and mushrooms on a tray and place under a hot grill for 5-7 minutes while you toast the bread. Place one piece of toast, four tomato halves and half the grilled mushrooms on each of two warm plates. Pour half the baked beans over each serving of toast and serve immediately.

Accompaniments
1 fresh orange per person
2 Oat Biscuits per person
Herbal tea

Traditional English Snack
3 Oat Biscuits per person
Herbal tea *or* mineral water

Traditional English Lunch

Salad Sandwiches
8 slices bread
2 teaspoons prepared mustard
1 medium cucumber, thinly sliced
8 lettuce leaves, washed

Accompaniments
2 Oat Biscuits per person
Herbal tea *or* mineral water

Traditional English Snack
3 Oat Biscuits per person
Herbal tea *or* mineral water

Traditional English Dinner

Pea Soup
8 oz/225g split green peas, washed and drained
2 cloves garlic, finely chopped (optional)
1 medium onion, peeled and finely chopped
2 tablespoons brewer's yeast
½ teaspoon ground coriander
freshly ground black pepper to taste

Place the split peas in a large saucepan and cover with twice their volume of water. Place the pan over a high heat and bring the liquid to a boil. (Split peas produce a lot of froth so ensure that you use an especially deep saucepan.) Add the remaining ingredients, stir well and reduce the heat to a medium setting. Cover the pan and leave the soup to simmer for 45 minutes. Reduce the heat if the liquid threatens to bubble over. Add more liquid if necessary, according to the thickness of soup you desire. Test the peas for tenderness after 45 minutes and cook for a further 15 minutes if necessary – the peas should be very tender and mushy. Serve hot.

Shepherd's Pie with Green Vegetables

8 oz/225g potatoes, scrubbed and cubed
1 tablespoon Marmite yeast extract (or low-salt equivalent)
1 medium onion, peeled and finely chopped
1 sachet/128g Protoveg TVP mince *or* chunks (or equivalent)
½ teaspoon dried thyme
½ teaspoon dried oregano
freshly ground black pepper to taste
4 oz/115g carrots, thinly sliced
6 oz/170g tin sweetcorn, drained
2 fl oz/60ml Plamil® soya milk concentrate
Green vegetables
8 oz/225g Brussels sprouts, trimmed and 'crossed'
8 oz/225g French beans, trimmed

Pre-heat the oven to 180°C/350°F (Gas Mark 4). Place the potatoes in a steamer and steam for 20 minutes, or until tender. Leave to cool in a mixing bowl.

Dissolve the yeast extract in 1 pint/570ml warm water. Pour a little of this liquid into a large frying pan and place over a high heat. When the liquid bubbles, add the onion and 'sauté' until the onion is tender, about 2-3 minutes. Add the TVP and the remaining liquid, stir well and continue to cook over a high to medium heat. When the TVP has softened and absorbed much of the liquid, add the herbs, pepper, carrots and sweetcorn. Stir well and remove from the heat. The mixture should not be dry, but slightly sloppy. Add more water if necessary.

Dilute the soya milk with 2 fl oz/60ml water. Mash the steamed potatoes in the mixing bowl, add the soya milk and a little black pepper if desired. Purée using a fork.

Turn the TVP and vegetable mixture into a casserole dish and spread the puréed potatoes over. Bake the pie for 30-40 minutes until it is cooked through and the potato has a lightly golden crust.

Meanwhile, steam the Brussels sprouts and French beans for 15 minutes, until tender. Turn into warmed serving dishes and serve immediately with the hot pie.

Banana Shake
(See recipe on page 94.)

Accompaniments
2 Oat Biscuits per person
Herbal tea

6
MORE WAYS TO CUT CHOLESTEROL

SOLUBLE FIBRE IS THE SECRET

There can hardly be a person left alive who hasn't heard of the benefits of eating a diet rich in fibre. Even so, some people still don't seem to have got the message – or at any rate, aren't acting upon it. In Britain alone, it is estimated by those people who make it their business to know about these things that four out of every ten people suffer from constipation, and two out of every ten suffer so severely that they have to use laxatives frequently. And yet, much of this heaving and straining could probably be prevented if only they ate a diet that was higher in natural forms of fibre!

One of the earliest advocates of the advantages of eating more natural fibre was Dr Denis Burkitt, who undertook much pioneering work in this area, and is recognized as one of the world's leading authorities on the subject. He once compared the diets of several different groups of people, ranging from rural Africans through to enlisted Naval seamen, and found a remarkable difference in the so-called 'transit time' (i.e. the average time it took for food to pass all the way through their bodies, from one end to the other). For rural Africans, and other groups such as vegetarians who ate a naturally high-fibre, high complex carbohydrate diet, the average transit time was in the region of thirty-six hours. But for those eating a low-fibre, high-fat diet (such as the seamen) the transit time was well over eighty hours! Apart from the obvious discomfort of constipation, this sort of transit time is unhealthy because it keeps toxins (including possible carcinogens) trapped inside the body long after they should have been expelled. But this isn't the only benefit that comes from eating a higher fibre diet. We asked Dr Burkitt to explain:

'There are basically two types of fibre, insoluble fibre and water-soluble fibre. The classic insoluble fibre is wheat fibre, with bran and all the bran products. That is highly effective for combating constipation, increasing stool weight, and preventing things like haemorrhoids and diverticular diseases. It's very good for the guts. But it does almost nothing for what we call the "metabolic diseases" associated with lack of fibre, particularly diabetes, and coronary heart disease. Now soluble fibre, on the other hand, does have an effect on combating constipation, but it *also* has an effect on lowering raised serum lipid [i.e. fats in your blood] levels, and also on glucose tolerance, so that it has a profoundly beneficial effect on diabetes. Now, as to *how* this fibre works in lowering the blood lipids, there are many suggestions. It has effects on bile acids and so on, but the main way in which soluble fibre is beneficial for diabetes is that it enormously slows down the absorption of energy from the gut. So instead of all the energy being absorbed, as it would be in sugar products, if you have a high-fibre product it makes the intestinal content into a sort of a gel, so that the energy is only absorbed into the circulation very slowly, and so you don't have great and sudden demands on insulin, and so on.'

From what Dr Burkitt says, you can see that *soluble* fibre is the sort to choose if you want to use it to lower your blood cholesterol level. But before you get too excited and eat all the soluble fibre within grabbing range, it is important to understand that only *certain forms* of soluble fibre seem to have this cholesterol-lowering effect. Not all soluble fibre seems to work like this. Unfortunately, some books and magazine articles don't make this sufficiently clear, and can leave you with the impression that *any* kind of soluble fibre should lower your cholesterol level. To try and understand more about this effect, we spoke to another world-recognized expert in his field, Dr David Southgate, a scientist who has had a method of dietary fibre analysis named after him – the 'Southgate Method'. This is what he told us:

'The first thing to understand, of course, is that not all soluble fibres have this effect. It looks as if the effect is related to the physical properties of the soluble fibre, and it seems as though you need a soluble fibre that produces a *viscous* [i.e. gluey] solution. A lot of the soluble materials in plant cell walls do produce viscous solutions, like pectin, guar gum and oat gum – they thicken the solution up and make it more viscous.

'Now, as for the mechanism whereby they do this, that's not really known for certain at the present time. But there are two theories as to how it might work. One is that it affects cholesterol metabolism by binding bile salts. Bile salts are cholesterol derivatives, and if you bind bile salts in the gut, you will prevent them from being re-absorbed lower down, thus affecting the metabolism of cholesterol in the liver.

'They may in fact work in that way, but there's no really clear evidence that some fibres do cause an increased excretion of bile salts and some don't. The other possible way that viscous, soluble fibres affect serum cholesterol is that these viscous materials can affect the absorption of *many* nutrients – they tend to slow the process of absorption down. In the case of fats and cholesterol it may lower the overall rate of absorption of cholesterol. By partially interfering with this process, it may produce its effect that way.

'It's not a simple story by any means. I think in the beginning, people hoped that it would be, but it doesn't look as if it is. In the whole area of dietary fibre research, there's always the added complication that most high-carbohydrate diets also tend to be low-fat diets as well. So some of the effects of a high-fibre diet may be a combination of the effects of not just eating more fibre, but also of lowering fat intake. Dietary fibre is such a complex mixture of different types of material, with different physical properties, that it's very difficult to generalize.'

So, although we don't yet know for certain precisely how viscous, soluble fibre manages to lower blood cholesterol, that really isn't so important. What we do know is that it *does seem to work*, and – equally importantly – a number of cheap and easy-to-obtain food-stuffs seem to contain important amounts of it. The rest of this chapter will explain where you can find good sources of viscous, soluble fibre, and also looks at some other substances which may have a cholesterol-lowering effect as well.

Insoluble Fibre	**Soluble Fibre**
Wheat Bran	Oat Bran
Wheat Germ	Pectin
Whole-Wheat Flour	Baked Beans

Food	Grams of soluble fibre in 100 g
Broccoli, frozen	13.36
Carrots, raw	11.32
Brussels sprouts, frozen	10.86
Cauliflower, frozen	8.92
Cabbage, raw	8.68
Spinach, frozen	6.56

OATS – THE GERM OF A GOOD IDEA

It was observed at least as long ago as 1963 that oats could have a cholesterol-lowering effect. However, it is only in recent years that, as part of the quest for the answer to coronary heart disease, scientists have again re-examined this humble and inexpensive product. Today, many experiments have shown that oat bran can and does act to significantly lower blood cholesterol. Here are the results of some recent, highly encouraging studies.

- Researchers at the University of California, Irvine, asked test subjects to eat two oat bran muffins a day over a month-long period. The results showed an average drop in total blood cholesterol of just over 5 per cent, and nearly a 9 per cent reduction in LDL (low density lipoprotein). There was also an 8 per cent cut in triglycerides.

- A report published in Scandinavia showed that a low-fat, low-cholesterol diet managed to reduce the blood cholesterol level of its subjects by 20 per cent. When foods containing soluble fibre (e.g. pulses, oats, fruits and vegetables) were added to the diet, an additional fall of 10 per cent serum cholesterol was observed.[30]

- When a group of eighteen healthy volunteers agreed to add either 23 grams of wheat bran or one 15 gram oat fibre tablet to their usual diet, the researchers found that the oat fibre was more effective in lowering both total cholesterol and LDL cholesterol. Interestingly, the 'beneficial' HDL (high density lipoprotein) level remained unchanged. 'The oat fibre tablet also proved easier to take and caused fewer side-effects', reported the scientists.[31]

- A group of twenty men with high blood cholesterol were admitted to a metabolic ward for twenty-one days. Some were fed a 'control' diet (with no oat bran) and others were fed exactly the same diet, but with added oat bran. After just three weeks, the men receiving oat bran supplementation had lowered their serum cholesterol concentrations by 19 per cent and had slashed their LDL concentrations by 23 per cent.[32]

- When eight men with hypercholesterolemia (high blood cholesterol) were fed 'control' and oat bran diets in alternation, it was found that while they were eating 100 grams of oat bran per day they managed to reduce their total serum cholesterol by 13 per cent, and LDL level by 14 per cent. HDL was not affected.[33]

- Scientists recruited volunteers from the Continental Illinois National Bank in Chicago to see whether adding oat bran to a low-fat diet could enhance its cholesterol-lowering effect. The experiment lasted twelve weeks, and, after four weeks on a restricted fat diet, half of them were told to add 56 grams of oat bran to their diets every day. After eight weeks of oat bran supplementation, their average blood cholesterol had dropped by about 10 per cent.[34]

In the above experiments, the actual amounts by which cholesterol drops seem to vary quite considerably. Of course, even a 5 per cent drop in your cholesterol level is worth achieving (remember the rule of thumb from Chapter One – 'for every 1 per cent drop in blood cholesterol, there is a 2 per cent drop in the risk of cardiovascular disease'). So even a 5 per cent decrease translates to a 10 per cent reduction in risk – which is well worth working for. In fact, the average range of total cholesterol reduction is in the region of 10-25 per cent, and probably depends to some extent on the degree of elevation of serum cholesterol to begin with, whether a low-fat diet is also being consumed at the same time, and how much oat bran is being consumed. A diet which includes about 100 grams of oat bran and lasts for at least three weeks (the longer the better) should show a useful improvement.

But are there any side-effects? Oats are a natural substance, which have been eaten for thousands of years, so any adverse reactions should be known by now. There may be a softening of your stools, which shouldn't be objectionable (it might be a welcome change!). You may have more wind, which should calm down after a short time. It is possible that, if you are taking more than 50 grams per day, some bloating or abdominal discomfort could occur, in which case you should reduce your intake and consult your doctor. As with all new diets, it would be advisable to consult your doctor prior to adding this amount of oat bran to your daily diet, so that your personal medical history can be taken into consideration. Perhaps the only real disadvantage is that it simply seems *too* easy. If you can achieve a useful reduction in blood cholesterol simply by adding oat bran to your normal food, then you may not take further steps to improve the rest of your diet. This would be a mistake. As Dr Basil Rifkind, chief of lipid metabolism and atherogenesis at the National Heart Lung and Blood Institute in Bethesda, says: 'It would be wrong for people to start consuming oat bran and forgetting about everything else. The main thing you want to do is increase complex carbohydrates in the diet and reduce the amount of fat you consume.'[35]

CORN BRAN

Just recently, there has been some speculation that corn bran (not as widely available as oat bran) may also be able to lower cholesterol. Researchers at Georgetown University Hospital found that when people ate raw corn bran their serum cholesterol was lowered by 20 per cent and triglycerides by 31 per cent. They gave about 40 grams daily to seven people suffering from hypercholesterolemia, and to make it palatable, flavoured it with garlic powder, black pepper and celery seed, and sprinkled it over tomato juice or soup. Apparently there were no serious side effects.

NIACIN

It has been known for some time that niacin – also called Vitamin
B3 – can lower cholesterol levels if taken in large amounts, and it is
probably one of the safest cholesterol-lowering drugs because of its
long track record. Niacin is naturally found in foods such as yeast,
milk, eggs, green vegetables and cereal grains, and your daily requirement of it comes to something in the region of 16 milligrams.
However, when used clinically to lower cholesterol, it is often
taken in doses which are enormously larger – 1-3 *grams* – almost
two hundred times the recommended daily allowance. Only niacin
in its nicotinic acid form has been found useful to lower cholesterol;
nicotinamide does not have the same effect.

In one study, thirty-seven patients (twenty-five male, twelve
female) with seriously high blood cholesterol were given both diet
therapy and niacin tablets. With diet therapy only, the average
cholesterol reduction was about 17 per cent, and although twelve
patients managed to get down to the goal of 5.2 millimoles, none of
them managed to maintain their cholesterol at that low level. On
the other hand, those patients receiving both diet therapy and niacin supplementation managed to reduce their average levels by 28
per cent, twenty-two of them reached the target level, and seven of
them succeeded in staying down there.[36]

For those people who suffer from very high blood cholesterol,
doctors sometimes prescribe niacin combined with one or more
other types of drug (perhaps something called a bile acid sequestrant, such as cholestyramine) and additional diet therapy. Under
these conditions, it is not uncommon to find a huge reduction in
cholesterol of 45-60 per cent!

You should remember, however, that your first line of attack
against cholesterol should be to reduce your total and saturated fat
and cholesterol intake, to control your weight, to increase your
physical activity, and to control any disease (such as diabetes or
hypothyroidism) which may be elevating your cholesterol. Drug
therapy should only be used when all these measures have failed,
and under the supervision of your doctor.

It is not known for sure how niacin works to reduce serum cholesterol – it is definitely metabolized in the liver, and probably ex-
erts its beneficial effect on the way your liver re-processes cholesterol and deals with LDL and VLDL. Also, niacin may partly
stop fatty tissues in other parts of the body from secreting fats.

When given in large doses, niacin also opens up blood vessels,
and this can cause something called the 'niacin flush' – an intense
reddening and itching of the face and upper body. Occasionally
it may also cause headache, nausea, dizziness, vomiting and

diarrhoea. The 'niacin flush' usually goes away after your body has been taking niacin for a couple of weeks. Slow-release niacin may minimize this effect in some people, which may be uncomfortable but is harmless.

Rarely, niacin may cause rapid beating of the heart. It may interfere with liver-function tests, and increase blood-sugar levels, which is important for diabetics because it may affect their medication requirement. It may also interfere with medications used for high blood pressure. Before you take niacin, tell your doctor if you have diabetes, coronary artery disease, gall-bladder disease or a history of jaundice or liver disease, gout, peptic ulcer or allergy. Tests to assess your liver's state of health may be necessary periodically.

Niacin is a useful and powerful weapon in our armoury against cholesterol, but like all weapons, it should be used at the right time and in the right hands. So speak to your doctor first.

BEANS

Beans can be just as effective as oat bran in lowering cholesterol, because they contain useful amounts of the same soluble fibre. 100 grams of oat bran contains nearly 8 grams of soluble fibre. By using the following table, you can see how several different types of beans compare.[37]

Food	Grams of soluble fibre in 100 g
Green beans, tinned	8.13
Navy beans, cooked	7.76
Pinto beans, cooked	7.52
Baked beans, tinned	6.3
Kidney beans, tinned	5.26

When researchers gave ten men suffering from hypercholesterolemia (high blood cholesterol) a diet containing half a cup of tinned beans every day for three weeks, they found that cholesterol levels had dropped by an average of 13 per cent and triglycerides had sunk by 12 per cent.[38] And this was on an 'average' diet which included a considerable amount of dietary fat and cholesterol! When British researchers carried out similar experiments, they also found that beans could cut cholesterol levels by about one-third.[39] The researchers used plain, ordinary tinned baked beans, and asked volunteers to eat one 500 gram tin a day. Within three days of starting, the subjects showed a 10-12 per cent drop in cholesterol! It seems, therefore, that eating some beans every day is a healthy, and easy, way to increase your cholesterol-loss.

GUAR GUM

Guar gum is made from the ground-up seed of the tree *cyamopsis tetragonolobus* (the tender cluster bean pod), and is used to bind pills and tablets together, and enables them to disintegrate on contact with moisture. It has also been used as a 'slimming pill', intended to be taken with water because it swells up in the stomach thus producing a feeling of fullness and, hopefully, a decreased appetite. However, there have been safety fears about its use in this manner, since it could swell up in the gullet causing a dangerous obstruction. Nevertheless, when used to reduce serum cholesterol levels, guar gum is known to be effective. When researchers studied fifty men, all of whom showed a moderately elevated cholesterol level, they found that after eight weeks' use, total cholesterol fell by an average of 1 millimole! The researchers found a greater decrease in cholesterol when using a high viscosity mixture rather than medium or low viscosity.[40]

In another experiment, scientists used diets enriched with both wheat bran and guar gum to produce cuts in total cholesterol and LDL ranging from 10-20 per cent, and found that these reductions applied equally to people with normal and elevated serum cholesterol readings.[41] The scientists concluded:

'Foods should be selected with moderate to high amounts of dietary fibre from a wide variety of choices to include both soluble and insoluble types of fibre. Insufficient data are available on the long-term safety of high-fibre supplements. People at risk of deficiencies, such as postmenopausal women, the elderly, or growing children, may require supplements of calcium and trace minerals. People with upper gastrointestinal dysfunction are at risk of bezoar formation and cautioned against a diet high in fibre of the leafy vegetable type.'

They also suggested that diabetics should pay careful attention to insulin doses, 'because hypoglycemia can result if there is a radical change in fibre intake and insulin dose is not reduced appropriately.'

A further experiment on fourteen volunteers, all of whom had been diagnosed as having hypercholesterolemia, produced a baffling result.[42] The experiment lasted twelve weeks, during which time the volunteers received daily supplements of 15 grams of guar gum. Half way through the trial, the results were very encouraging – showing an average reduction of about 1 millimole, about a 12 per cent drop. But after this midway point, the cholesterol levels began to climb again, and at the end of the trial, there was no difference. Puzzling though this is, there was at least one encouraging result – the scientists observed no severe side effects during the course of the experiment, and calcium, magnesium, phosphate, and iron levels in the body were not affected by guar gum supplementation. However, another study also using 15 grams of guar gum supplementation a day *did* find a sustained reduction after three months, although the average drop in total cholesterol was rather modest – about half a millimole, or 5 per cent.[43]

One of the largest reductions in cholesterol due to guar gum supplementation we could discover occurred in nineteen patients diagnosed as being hypercholesterolemic, who received guar gum every day, and who averaged a 15 per cent reduction in serum cholesterol after three months' treatment. The reduction was maintained after a year on the supplement, and the fall in LDL was 20 per cent on average. There was no reduction in triglycerides, nor in 'good' HDL. Two patients had to withdraw from the experiment because of severe diarrhoea.[44]

PECTIN

Pectin is made from apples or citrus fruits, and is the gelling agent used to make fruit jams and jellies. It has also been used to treat diarrhoea. Like guar gum and oat bran, pectin is a good source of soluble fibre, and has demonstrated its ability to lower serum cholesterol. In one trial, six men with familial hypercholesterolemia were alternately treated with diet therapy plus cholestyramine (cholesterol-lowering drug), and diet therapy, cholestyramine and additional pectin. After eight weeks on each regime, it was found that with pectin added, total serum cholesterol was lowered by 31 per cent and LDL fell by 35 per cent. This was an improvement of 20 per cent above and beyond the effect of diet and cholestyramine alone. The amount of pectin added was quite small – 12 grams a day, or about one scant tablespoon.[45] In another experiment, volunteers were given a daily dose of 15 grams of pectin combined with 450 milligrams of ascorbic acid (Vitamin C) for six weeks, at the end of which it was found that their total serum cholesterol had fallen by more than 8 per cent.[46] In the same trial, it was noticed that for other subjects suffering from more severe hypercholesterolemia, the drop was more pronounced – up to 18 per cent.

Pectin is probably a useful adjunct to the dietary control of cholesterol, and since a small amount seems to produce a beneficial effect, one tablespoon a day could be easily incorporated into most diets.

PSYLLIUM

Psyllium seeds (from the *psyllium plantain,* sometimes called ispaghula) have been used in bulk laxative preparations because when wettened, they swell up into a viscous mass, stimulating intestinal activity. There is also evidence that psyllium, like some other gel-producing gums, can act favourably on blood cholesterol levels. Twenty-six men were recruited by researchers, who gave them 3½ grams of psyllium at mealtimes, three times a day. No other dietary restrictions were imposed. After eight weeks of treatment, total cholesterol levels had fallen by nearly 15 per cent, and LDL had dropped by 20 per cent. The researchers observed no adverse effects, and concluded that 'psyllium is an effective and well-tolerated therapy for mild to moderate hypercholesterolemia'.[47] In another trial, fibre made from psyllium husks was given to twelve elderly patients for four months, after which time it was found that blood cholesterol had dropped by 20 per cent, but triglycerides were not lowered.[48]

However, some adverse reactions have been noted following psyllium usage, including allergic reaction (anaphylaxis)[49] and hypersensitivity leading to anaphylactic shock.[50] You should therefore check with your doctor if you notice any unusual symptoms if you use psyllium, and should avoid it if you are likely to be allergic.

BETA FIBRE

'Beta Fibre' is a completely new soluble fibre product, made from the sugar beet after the sugar has been extracted. As part of an experiment to test its effectiveness, twelve healthy volunteers ate half a loaf of bread every day for two weeks. Some ate loaves to which guar gum had been added, and others ate Beta Fibre supplemented loaves. Those taking guar gum experienced a 12 per cent fall in total cholesterol, those on Beta Fibre fell by 5 per cent. The fall, although relatively small compared to some pharmaceutical cholesterol-lowering agents was consistent and a more pronounced effect was seen when it was consumed by people with higher than healthy cholesterol levels.

One of the major advantages is the ease with which Beta Fibre can be included in a wide range of foods. It contains 50 per cent soluble fibre together with about 25 per cent insoluble fibre and is a dry powder which can be used in cooking with minimal effect on the taste and texture. Like all dry fibre supplements it must not be consumed in its dry state.

WELCOME TO YOUR NEW LIFE!

Congratulations on completing the Quick Cholesterol Clean-Out! We hope that you have noticed a number of beneficial changes in the way you feel during the time you have followed it. Now, to get some concrete indication of how successful the diet has been in reducing your cholesterol level, we suggest that you return to your doctor and get your blood cholesterol measured again. In fact, we recommend that you make the appointment during the final week of your diet so that you can measure any reduction immediately you have completed the six-week programme. If your triglycerides were measured in your initial test, you should repeat that test as well. And we suggest that, while you are there, you get your weight and blood pressure checked once more.

In a moment we will give your general dietary and lifestyle guidelines that will help you to maintain the reduced level of cholesterol in your blood. Before we do that however, a further word on testing. Although your cholesterol level, once reduced, can be maintained at a low level by making small but permanent alterations to your diet, we recommend that you test it again in one year's time. This will give you an opportunity to see your progress or, conversely, to make further corrections to your diet to maintain a healthy blood cholesterol level. If you are happy with the results of the one-year-later test, it would still be sensible to have your blood cholesterol level checked once every five years.

TONGUE TWISTERS

You may remember that in Chapter Four we advised that you follow the Quick Cholesterol Clean-Out for six weeks, if possible. We said that this period of time is generally long enough to enable you to establish new dietary habits. Well, we think that it is also just long enough for new dietary *tastes* to emerge.

You probably don't remember being a baby of two years or younger, but it is said of babies that they have 'pure palates' which are extremely sensitive to salt, sugar and other tastes which adults find normal, or even bland. Something happens, of course, between babydom and adulthood to taint the tastebuds, or at least dull their responses. Aging is part of the reason, but much of the blame must also be given to the foods we choose to eat. Meals abundant in salt, sugar and fats have a powerful effect that seems to numb the tastebuds to more subtle flavours which babies, for instance, enjoy. These powerful foods eventually create a taste habit which some people even describe as a craving. When these people eat food without these 'tongue tranquillizers', they will probably find the flavours disappointing, or even non-existent.

Six weeks following a low-salt, low-sugar, low-fat diet lets your tastebuds rejuvenate and perform the really high-quality work they are designed to do. Suddenly, foods that previously seemed only vehicles for very strong flavours can be enjoyed for their *real* flavour. Raw and 'plain' foods reveal themselves as exceptionally tasty, even aromatic, without any help from the usual lashings of salt, sugar and fat.

You may find that during the first few days of the Quick Cholesterol Clean-Out, your food seems bland. We suggest that you do two things: have patience and, if you want very strong flavours, explore the many herbs and spices that can be added to most meals. However, we feel certain that by the end of your diet you, too, will re-experience the clean palate of your youth which can revolutionize your attitude towards and enjoyment of the wholesome foods which offer you health. You'll probably also find that stale, greasy, fatty food somehow loses its appeal. Too bad!

THE CHOLESTEROL CONTROL DIET

It is possible that, as well as reducing your blood cholesterol level, the Quick Cholesterol Clean-Out could benefit you in a number of other ways. For instance, you could experience a normalization in blood pressure or weight, a decrease in the number of headaches and other general aches you suffer, and a relief from problems like constipation, lack of energy and poor skin. Will all these ailments return, then, at the end of six weeks? We don't think they need to.

It is possible to make permanent adjustments to your everyday diet that will keep it in line with those features of the Quick Cholesterol Clean-Out which brought you one or more of the health benefits listed above. We offer a set of guidelines now that will help you to keep the health you have gained and keep cardiovascular risk to a minimum.

> **A diet to control the level of cholesterol in your blood**
>
> ● Eat a minimum of eight Special Oat Biscuits each day.
> ● Eat a minimum of 1 lb (455g) of dried beans or lentils each week.
> ● Eat a fresh fruit, vegetable or fruit and vegetable salad each day, weighing at least 1 lb (455g).
> ● Eat two or three servings of a whole-grain food each day.
> ● Keep your daily intake of total fat to about 20 per cent of your total calorie intake, with only one-third of this amount as saturated fat.
> ● Use olive or safflower oils when adding fat to your meals.
> ● Keep your intake of dietary cholesterol to a minimum.

Getting Your Oats

Oat bran is a very important feature of the Quick Cholesterol Clean-Out because the type of soluble fibre it contains helps to reduce your cholesterol level. We don't think you should be without it so we suggest that you continue to eat our Special Oat Biscuits every day. However, instead of the compulsory twelve biscuits per day included in the six-week diet period, you may reduce your consumption to eight Special Oat Biscuits per day. Of course, you may eat twelve if you like! Simply, eight should provide you enough of the soluble fibre to keep your cholesterol level under control.

Beans on Toast

Most members of the legumes and pulses group of foods also contain the soluble fibre so effective at reducing cholesterol levels. We recommend that you continue to eat from this food group on a regular, if not daily, basis. Specifically, we think that you should eat a minimum of 1 lb (455g) *dried* beans or lentils each week. This amount translates (cooked, of course) into a very easy-to-eat meal plan. For instance, approximately ¼ lb (115g) dried white beans is contained in a 1 lb (455g) tin of baked beans in tomato sauce. In which case, four servings of beans on toast per week does the job! That is only one of many beany options, however. Lentil soup, dhal, fagioli and many other bean recipes, some included in this book, will help to boost your supply of that precious soluble fibre. So get into beans!

Salad Days

While we are still talking about what you *should* eat, let's consider the humble salad. As you know, fresh fruits and vegetables are very rich in vitamins and minerals – especially if they are really fresh, or even organically grown. In addition, they supply a great deal of insoluble fibre, also known as 'roughage' which can relieve constipation and other digestive ills. We recommend that you eat a salad that weighs at least 1 lb (455g) every day. It can be entirely fruit, entirely vegetable, or a combination of the two to create a colourful and richly textured salad. Please enjoy and experiment with the dozens of fruits and vegetables available the year round.

Going With the Grain

The cereal group of foods should also be an important part of your long-term diet, especially those grains that have not been over-processed and so lost much of their nutrient value. We have used the term 'whole grain' to describe these cereals, which include rice, barley, oats, wheat and many others found on the shelves of supermarkets and health food shops. Many staples, such as bread, are widely available made from whole cereals. Whole grains are especially rich in vitamins, minerals, carbohydrate and insoluble fibre. We recommend that you have two to three servings of whole-grain food each day. These may be in the form of whole-grain breads, rice, couscous, millet, whole-wheat pasta and porridge – just to name a few.

Putting Fat on the Fire

Throughout the six-week diet period, your total dietary fat intake was kept at 20 per cent, or less, of your total calorie intake – approximately *half* of the average daily intake. We recommend that you continue to keep your intake of fat at – or very near to – this reduced level. Furthermore, we suggest a few changes to the types of fat you choose and the way in which you eat them.

Saturated fat should comprise no more than one-third of your total fat intake (about 7 per cent of your total calories). We have found that this is easily achieved because a small amount of saturated fat is present in a number of plant foods and quickly adds up to this recommended amount. However, that doesn't leave much room for foods such as meat, dairy products, coconut oil and eggs, so we recommend you avoid these foods when eating to control your cholesterol level.

The remainder of your fat allowance should come from unsaturated fats, which are derived from plant foods. Unsaturated fats (these are either polyunsaturated or mono-unsaturated) usually remain liquid at room temperature, therefore this part of your fat intake comes from the wide selection of plant oils available. We recommend two oils in particular.

First, **olive oil** which is a mono-unsaturated fat. It has been found useful in the control of cholesterol, which is why we favour using it. In one trial, it was found that adding olive oil to the diet lowered total cholesterol by nearly 10 per cent, cut LDL by 12 per cent, and reduced total triglycerides by 25 per cent. Most remarkable, however, is that it *didn't* affect the level of 'good' HDL circulating in the blood![51] The scientists concluded that 'Olive oil may be a natural fat that can be used for the control of plasma and LDL cholesterol as a valid alternative to polyunsaturated fatty acids.' Another even more remarkable study compared two different types of diet – one a complex carbohydrate diet, rich in plant food, and the other rich in olive oil.[52] The results were indeed stunning. The researchers found that serum cholesterol levels fell on average by 0.44 millimoles in those eating the complex carbohydrate diet, and *also* fell by 0.46 millimoles in the olive oil group! 'Good' HDL levels fell by 0.19 millimoles in the carbohydrate group, but *rose* by 0.03 millimoles in the olive oil group! 'These results,' wrote the researchers, 'clearly show that the olive-oil-rich diet, unlike the complex-carbohydrate-rich diet, caused a specific fall in non-HDL cholesterol while leaving serum triglyceride levels virtually unchanged.'

This effect is sometimes referred to as the 'Mediterranean' effect, because olive oil is such a prominent part of the diet of many Mediterranean peoples, who suffer much less from atherosclerosis and coronary heart disease. Although we don't suggest you do anything to *increase* your total fat consumption, it does seem as if it would be a prudent step to reduce your saturated fat intake where you can, and to replace it with a mono-unsaturated type such as olive oil. We have also found that olive oil is a very satisfying component of the diet: if you are going to use an oil, why not use a really high-quality one that also has a unique flavour and aroma? In fact, we no longer buy margarine for our meals. On the occasions when we have toast for breakfast, for instance, we have taken to spreading the slices with a very little olive oil – using a basting brush to make the job easier. It's delicious! Do buy a cold-pressed olive oil, however: it is more nutritious, has more flavour and, though it costs more, works out as excellent value for money because you don't need to use much to enjoy it.

Secondly, **safflower oil** contains a high percentage of a fatty acid called *linoleic acid*. This fatty acid is essential to your health and can only be derived from the diet – you can't make it in your body. It is possible that linoleic acid could actually help to reduce cholesterol in your blood. Safflower oil contains more linoleic acid than any of the other widely available oils (about 10 grams in 1 tablespoon of oil)[53] – which is why we recommend it. Buy this oil cold-pressed as well.

As you may have noticed from the recipes, we have dropped oil and fats from most stages of meal preparation. Frying is completely out of the picture and techniques such as sauté and stir-fry take on a new meaning. (See the Glossaries for details of the methods we use instead.) We think you'll enjoy the new flavours which these simple changes create, and which help create long-term good health.

Cholesterol Counting – The Easy Way

While it's not too difficult to follow a short six-week diet programme (especially with the delicious recipes and quick snacks we've included for you in this book!), we do understand that it is simply unrealistic to expect *anyone* to follow a precise diet programme for the rest of their lives. Christmas, holidays, birthdays, business lunches, wedding anniversaries ... they're all occasions when it becomes difficult or impossible to stick to a diet. Well, we've given this problem a great deal of thought, and we believe that we've found a unique solution which will allow you to choose from a *huge* variety of food, and *still* eat a healthy, low-cholesterol diet!

Until now, it's been next-to-impossible to find a quick way to decide which foods you should eat and which ones to avoid while still exercising firm control over your cholesterol level. But now, *The Quick Cholesterol and Fat Counter*[54] can help you to do just this. It contains guidance on three thousand common food items, and should be your constant companion wherever you go. For the first time ever, it's easy to keep track of the cholesterol and the saturated fat in the food you eat. It will allow you the freedom to choose the right food, and avoid the wrong ones. In many ways, it is your 'passport to freedom', because it lets *you* choose which foods you want to eat, rather than obliging you to eat a fixed menu. It comes with quick and easy instructions, and we know it will be a great help to cholesterol counters everywhere!

WHAT ABOUT THE REST OF YOUR LIFE?

Well, we hope it's a long and healthy one! However, you may be wondering when you can 'stop dieting' and go back to your 'normal' food. Our answer is: any time. You, and most other people living in western countries, are in the fortunate position of being able to eat almost anything you like. Furthermore, you can eat almost any *amount* of anything you like, even until you burst, if that's the way you want to go. But why should you? It is now widely accepted in medical circles that dietary excesses such as we 'enjoy' in Britain are, in fact, killing us. Presumably you have realized that your own life has suffered, or was in danger of suffering, as a result of such dietary indiscretions. So, also presumably, you decided to act, to set it right, to improve your chances of living a bit longer.

We think that is wonderful. You have shown that you value your life and we know from experience that, once you face up to that feeling, you will never act or think in quite the same way again. And thank goodness! Now you can *really* begin to shape the future you want for yourself and your family. You are in *control* again and that control starts with your body and your health. You have a fresh opportunity to improve your health and fine-tune your body so that you may fully enjoy the years you have ahead of you.

Maybe you can understand, now, why we say 'you *must*' do this or that and why we don't refer to this programme as 'dieting'. Instead, we call it a way of life. It is a personal celebration of life through food and eating; an approach to health that involves other life forms and, as such, ought really to command a profound and respectful relationship between yourself and the food you select. We feel certain you will select wisely and we wish you a very long, very healthy life – one full of good food and happiness!

GLOSSARIES

1. A BRIEF A-Z OF MEDICAL WORDS

Anaphylactic shock (anaphylaxis) A severe and unusual allergic reaction to a substance.

Anemia A shortage of red blood cells, and therefore haemoglobin, in your blood.

Aneurysm A weak point in the wall of an artery which bulges and may burst, or rupture.

Angina (pectoris) A distinct, gripping pain in the chest indicating that the muscle of your heart is not receiving enough oxygen.

Arteriole A very small branch of artery which connects to the capillaries.

Artery The channel, or vessel, which carries blood away from your heart.

Atherogenisis The formation of atheroma, and its consequent damage, in the arteries.

Atheroma From the Greek, meaning 'porridge'. Atheroma is the mixture of fat, blood and calcium which builds up in deposits along the artery walls.

Atherosclerosis A hardening and narrowing of the arteries due to build-up of atheroma.

Atrium (plural=atria) The 'waiting rooms' of your heart. The two upper chambers of your heart which collect blood prior to it being pumped out of the heart again.

Bezoar A solid lump of matter, often of hair, fruit or vegetable origin, in the stomach or intestine which develops over a period of time.

Bile A fluid secreted by the liver which plays an essential part in the absorption of fats.

Blood Pressure The pressure of blood against your artery walls.

Calcification A feature of advanced atherosclerosis, the addition of calcium to the deposits (atheroma), causing them to harden.

Calorie A measure of a unit of heat or energy. Food converts into energy and the amount of energy each food gives is measured in calories.

Capillaries Tiny vessels connecting the arterioles and venules which form a dense network throughout the body.

Carbon Monoxide A very poisonous gas present in car exhaust and cigarette smoke.

Carboxy-haemoglobin The substance which takes the place of oxygen in the red blood cell in those who smoke. Carbon monoxide combines with haemoglobin to create carboxy-haemoglobin.

Cardiac Having to do with the heart.

Cardiovascular Having to do with the heart and blood vessels.

Cerebrovascular Having to do with the brain and the blood vessels. In particular with the supply of blood to the brain.

Cholesterol A fatty substance found in all animal fats.

Chylomicron A droplet of fluid which transports fats and cholesterol from the intestine. It contains triglycerides, cholesterol, phospholipids and protein.

Coronary Relating to the heart. Some people say 'he's had a coronary' when referring to someone who has had a heart attack.

Coronary Heart Disease A term used to describe the group of symptoms which result from diseased coronary arteries. These include angina, heart attack and sudden death.

Coronary Thrombosis A coronary artery blocked by a blood clot.

Diastole The lowest blood pressure reading. From the point in your heart beat when the heart muscle is relaxed.

Embolism Blockage of an artery (usually quite sudden) by a break-away atheroma deposit, blood clot or foreign body.

Erythrocytes Red blood cells.

Fatty Acid The substances in fat that give it its unique flavour, texture and melting point.

Glucose Also called blood sugar, this is the final product from your body's breakdown of carbohydrate food.

Haemoglobin The pigment of your red blood cells, containing iron, which carries oxygen and carbon dioxide.

Haemorrhage An abnormal discharge of blood, internally or externally.

Hardening of the Arteries The process of atherosclerosis with calcification.

HDL High-density lipoprotein.

Heart Attack *see* Myocardial Infarction.

Hormone A chemical secreted by your glands which travels through your tissue fluid to an organ where it triggers a specific effect on your metabolism.

Hypercholesterolemia High blood cholesterol.

Hypersensitivity An exaggerated reaction to a foreign substance.

Hypertension Abnormally high blood pressure.

Hypocholesterolemic Having the effect of lowering the level of cholesterol in the blood.

Infarct An area of dead tissue, or scar tissue. An infarction is the death of tissue due to loss of oxygen supply.

Insoluble Fibre Not able to be dissolved in water. Also called 'roughage', this type of fibre is contained in such foods as wheat bran.

Ischaemic (Heart Disease) Having to do with lack of blood supply, therefore causing lack of oxygen supply.

LDL Low-density lipoprotein.

Leucocytes White blood cells.

Lipid A fat substance.

Lipoprotein A combination of fat (lipids) and protein which enables lipids to be transported in a water-soluble medium (blood).

Metabolism The chemical process of assimilating food by turning it into energy and substances which will repair and replace body tissues. Your metabolism includes all of the stages and features of this process.

Myocardial Infarction Also known as heart attack. The death of heart muscle after its supply of blood, and therefore oxygen, has been interrupted.

Myocardium The heart muscle itself. The muscle wall of the heart.

Niacin Also known as vitamin B3.

Obesity The state of being overweight by 15 per cent or more of your optimum body weight.

Plasma The liquid element of the blood, in which all particles are suspended to form blood.

Platelets Small structures found in the blood whose chief role is in the clotting and coagulation of blood.

Sequestrant A substance which binds. An example is Cholestyramine, a substance used in drug treatment of high cholesterol, which binds bile acids in your intestine and aids in their excretion.

Serum The clear fluid element of plasma which remains when all the particles have been removed from it.

Soluble Fibre Fibre that is water-soluble. Of especial importance in cholesterol reduction is the type of soluble fibre that is gluey or viscous in nature.

Stroke A cerebrovascular accident. Damage to an area of brain due to the blockage or rupture of a blood vessel in the brain.

Supplement A substance given in addition to your diet in order to enhance its nutritional value.

Systole The highest blood pressure reading. From the point in your heart beat when your heart muscle is contracting, or pumping.

Thrombus (Thrombosis) A blood clot. Thrombosis is the formation of a blood clot.

Tissue Cells of a particular kind which group together for a specific function, i.e. muscle tissue, skin tissue, bone tissue.

Toxic Having the effect of a poison. The amount of a substance which may be toxic will vary depending on individual tolerances for it.

Triglyceride A fat made from carbohydrates and stored in your body tissues.

Vascular Having to do with blood vessels or blood supply.

Veins Blood vessels or channels that return blood to the heart.

Ventricle (plural=ventricles) The two lower chambers of the heart which pump blood out of the heart into the arteries.

Viscous Glutinous.

VLDL Very low-density lipoprotein.

2. NOTES ON INGREDIENTS INCLUDED IN OUR RECIPES

All Bran® Cereal Although a brand-name product, there are many similar breakfast cereals on the market should you prefer. Buy them in any supermarket or health-food store. All Bran® is high in fibre, very filling, sustaining and rich in vitamins and minerals.

Bread and Flour These are not used a great deal in these recipes. Where they are, however, we recommend that you use whole-grain bread and flour. Whole-wheat bread and flour is the most widely available, but it is increasingly easy to purchase rye or mixed-grain breads and flours that use the whole grain – always more nutritious and higher in fibre.

Brewer's Yeast This is a very broad heading for a variety of dry yeast products widely available in both supermarkets and health-food shops. Brewer's yeast is perhaps the most well known and, although sold originally in semi-liquid form, we intend you to use the dry or powdered form which is also 'de-bittered'. There are many other yeast products available, however, and an increasing number of these are low in salt – specifically, Engevita Nutritional Yeast Flakes, and Comvita Unsalted Food Yeast. Yeast products are rich in the B group of vitamins as well as protein and a number of trace minerals. They add a subtle flavour to your food, one that complements the other ingredients in the dish. The amounts recommended are used to enhance sauces and gravies, but you may discover other dishes to which you may add 1-2 tablespoons of brewer's yeast each day.

Bulgar This is a whole-grain wheat product, famous in Middle Eastern cooking. Most supermarkets have it, though they may market it as cracked wheat. If you don't find it, try *couscous* or *pourgouri* instead, both of which are popular as well as similar in texture, flavour and cooking method to bulgar.

Cider Vinegar This is a natural food with possible health benefits attributed to it. It is easy to find in either supermarkets or health-food shops, where it may even be purchased in an organic form. Use as much as you like, more than these recipes call for if that suits your taste.

Dried Fruits We have included prunes, figs, dates and raisins in these recipes. All of them are available in supermarkets and health-food shops. We recommend that you try to find sun-dried varieties that are not coated in sugar – more and more shops are stocking fruits of this sort. Dried fruits are naturally sweet and rich in minerals. Most need a quick wash before they are used.

Egg Replacer This product is available under a number of brand names from major supermarkets and health-food shops. It is entirely free of eggs or their derivatives and may be used in most recipes that require eggs for binding or raising purposes. We have included it only in the Special Oat Biscuit recipe but you may find it becomes a permanent feature in your cupboard, especially for use in baking.

Frozen Foods Most of the vegetables called for in these recipes may be purchased in frozen form. Peas, carrots, corn, beans, Brussels sprouts and many others are easy to find in any supermarket or frozen food centre. By all means use these foods if you like as they are very convenient and make meal preparation exceptionally quick. However, fresh food is usually richer in nutrients than frozen or tinned food and we will always recommend that you use fresh food when possible.

Herbs and Spices In their fresh form many herbs and spices are rich in vitamins and minerals. Fresh parsley is an excellent example of a nutrient-rich fresh herb. In their dried form, some of the nutrients are lost, while the flavours tend to become more concentrated. We have listed specific amounts of most of the herbs and spices included, with occasional instructions to use them 'to taste'. In fact, you should feel free to explore the very wide range of herbs and spices available and to use them according to your preference. They will make little effect on the nutritional outcome of your meal, but may greatly affect your enjoyment of it!

Marmite This is a yeast extract in a paste form. Marmite is the most familiar brand and is available at all supermarkets. However, it is very high in salt and for this reason you may wish to discover the other low-salt brands available. A visit to a health-food shop is called for, where a variety of yeast products are available, as well as vegetable extracts that are low in salt but otherwise closely resemble Marmite. Some excellent examples are Barmene, Tastex, Vecon and Natex. All yeast products are rich in the B group of vitamins, protein and a number of trace minerals.

Molasses This is a by-product of sugar production so it is very sweet. However, it is also rich in the B vitamins, iron and other minerals. We include it in a few recipes to add nutritional value, flavour and sweetness. You may reduce the amounts called for if you wish.

Oat Bran and Germ This product is available under the Prewett's, Mornflake or Quaker Oats brand names, available from most supermarkets and all health-food shops. It should be stored in an airtight container in a cool place, such as your refrigerator. It is inexpensive, very nutritious and one of the foods most important in lowering cholesterol levels in your blood.

Pasta This is very popular and easy to find. We recommend that you check the label to make sure the pasta you buy is made without eggs, as eggs are very high in cholesterol. A quick stroll through our local supermarket revealed four different varieties of eggless pasta – so you will have no trouble finding this food.

Plamil® Soya Milk Available in dilute or concentrated form, this is one of the best soya milks on the market. We have chosen it because it is free of cholesterol as well as fortified with Vitamins B12 and D, to help meet your daily requirements for these nutrients. The concentrated form is listed in these recipes because it has a very pleasing taste and 'mouth feel' and may also resemble cream, for those who like that particular food.

We have given our recommendations for dilution ratios, but you may suit yourself and add as much or as little water as you like. Plamil is available from health-food shops. You will find that most supermarkets stock soya milk, should you wish to use another brand. However, some of these may not be fortified with Vitamins B12 and D.

Vitamin D is essential to health. Although an exact requirement has not been established, the Department of Health and Social Security has recommended a daily intake of 2.5mcg of Vitamin D for adults (not including pregnant or lactating women). Most, if not all, of this amount can be met by ensuring that you have 15 minutes of sunlight on your face and hands each day. In Britain, 'sunlight' may be taken as 'skylight' such as is common on cloudy days. However, many food products are fortified with this vitamin to ensure that your needs, and the needs of children and pregnant and lactating women, are met. Plamil Soya Milk is one such product.

Protoveg This is a brand name product using Texturized Vegetable Protein (TVP). TVP is made from soybeans and is processed into a high protein, low-fat food made to resemble the texture of some meat products. It is highly versatile as it comes in mince and chunk form, plain and various 'meaty' flavours (beef, chicken, bacon), and will conform to the other flavours and textures you want from your meal. Most supermarkets and all health-food shops sell this brand or an equivalent TVP product. In fact, many shops, such as Boots, package their own TVP. Other vegetable protein products (from ingredients other than TVP) include Vege-Burger, VegeBanger, Dietburger and the Granose or Lotus range of products. Experiment until you find a TVP or vegetable protein product that you are happy with.

The Protoveg recommended in these recipes provides a very high-protein nutritional profile as well as a fairly filling dish. Should you wish to reduce the quantities called for, by all means do so – just be aware that your protein intake for that day will drop. Each TVP or vegetable protein product has its own hydration instructions, but in general the ratio is two parts water to one part TVP. So if you reduce the amount of TVP in your meal, reduce the liquid accordingly.

Red Lentils and Green Split Peas These may be purchased in any supermarket. We include them because, not only are they full of fibre, vitamins and minerals, they are also the quickest of the legumes and pulses to prepare. Neither of these require soaking or pressure cooking and you can make a soup from them within 30-40 minutes.

Rice We recommend you to use brown rice when possible as this is more nutritious than white or 'instant' rices. It takes longer to cook, so you may have to alter your cooking schedule somewhat; an alternative is to use basmati rice, which is very tasty, aromatic and quick to cook. Both brown and basmati rice are available at all supermarkets and health-food stores. Of course, white rice is perfectly acceptable in all recipes that include rice, if you prefer its flavour and texture.

Tinned Foods We have included a number of tinned foods in the recipes to help keep the preparation of these meals as quick and easy as possible. You will note that we have also recommended low-salt varieties beside many tinned foods. Many manufacturers currently market low-salt versions of their products because public interest in health has increased over the last five years. We recommend that you select these in preference to the high-salt versions. All supermarkets and all health-food shops have a selection for you to choose from.

The precise weight of the tinned food may vary from brand to brand. Therefore you may use the weights listed in the recipes as approximations and purchase the size tin closest to that recommended.

Beans Most tinned beans have been pre-cooked. Check the label to make sure. We have included tinned kidney beans, chickpeas, white beans (haricot, butter or other) and, of course, baked beans in tomato sauce. If you prefer, you may always cook beans yourself from their raw state using a pressure cooker to do the job quickly while preserving nutrients.

Tomatoes Every cupboard should have a few tins! Whether purée, paste, chopped or whole, tinned tomatoes are a backbone to much of the cooking we do in this country. Our only recommendation is that you seek out low-salt varieties, as tinned tomatoes can be, unnecessarily, very high in salt.

Bamboo Shoots We have listed an 8 oz/225g tin. You may find larger or smaller sizes in your supermarket or even your local greengrocer. Bamboo shoots are not high in fats or calories so you may remain flexible and use whatever size tin is available.

Others Sweetcorn and green peas are among the other tinned foods you may wish to have on hand. Every supermarket has them, and all you need do is avoid those brands high in salt and sugar. Peas are notorious for having colouring added to them, so we recommend you avoid these brands as well. Of course, many foods are available in tins, even those basic foods such as potatoes and carrots. Our feeling is that, where possible, fresh food is always best but that, for those rare occasions when you just don't have the time, tinned food is a useful standby.

Tofu This is often called 'bean curd' because it is made from soy beans. The beans are made into milk and the milk into tofu, in a process similar to making cheese. Tofu is widely available in both supermarkets and health-food shops. Most supermarkets stock the 'silken' variety which is a soft tofu. Some of these recipes call for a firm tofu which you are certain to find in a health-food shop. There are a great many brand names and you may try them all until you find the brand you are happiest with. Every manufacturer makes a recognizably different tofu, so if you don't like the first type you try, move on to another!

Tofu is very low in fat, contains no cholesterol and is high in protein and minerals. It is a light, versatile food that, though bland by itself, may be prepared as a vehicle for other flavours.

Tostadas These are made from corn (maize) in a similar way to the Indian pappadam. They are low in calories and fats with a distinct flavour and texture. Most large supermarkets and some health-food shops stock these. Taco shells are the same product, but simply folded!

3. USEFUL UTENSILS

Here are some kitchen utensils that are very useful for making the change to healthy cooking.

Food Processor This is a versatile piece of equipment that speeds up most natural food preparation. A wide range of processors exist, and each offers a set of blades and attachments that perform slicing, dicing, mixing, puréeing, shredding and grating in less time than it takes to talk about it. They are noisy and they do need cleaning afterwards, but they also enable you to produce a salad, sauce or pâté in a matter of minutes.

Blender This is a large jug with a blade attachment in the bottom that sits on an electric motor. It may come with your food processor but, if it doesn't, we recommend you get one for those milk shakes, dips and sauces you will be making. The depth of the jug means that you can make a very liquid mixture without worrying about it spilling over the centre opening – as can happen with some food processors.

Universal Steamer This is a perforated basket whose sides are made of adjustable leaves of stainless steel so that it may fit most pan sizes. It is placed in a pan which contains an inch or so of water. The vegetables are placed in the steamer, the pan is covered and the whole is placed over the heat. Steaming is an alternative to boiling vegetables; it is as quick as boiling but leaves more of the flavour and nutrition in your food. Plastic steamers are available for microwave cooking. Please avoid using aluminium steamers.

Pressure Cooker This is a quick and efficient way of cooking beans and pulses while keeping their nutritional value. Food is cooked with very little water in a sealed pan so that the steam created is kept under pressure. Vegetables may also be cooked in this way, although the saving in time is not nearly so great as when cooking beans. A stainless steel pressure cooker is preferable to an aluminium version.

NOTE: We will take this opportunity to recommend that you gradually eliminate your stock of aluminium pans – unless they are enamel coated. Aluminium is known to be toxic to the human body and, unfortunately, pans made from this metal may pass some toxicity into the foods they contain. Instead, use stainless steel, enamel coated, glass or iron pans. (Iron pans actually increase the amount of iron in your diet.) Non-stick pans are also recommended, especially as they help reduce the quantity of oil needed in cooking.

4. COOKING METHODS

The way you cook your food is often as important to its ultimate nutritional value as the type of food you buy in the first place. Many cookery methods cause great loss of nutrients and some methods even turn a healthy food into an unhealthy one. Here are methods which preserve the quality of your food.

Steaming Use a universal steamer, as described above, to cook your vegetables quickly but without losing nutrients or texture. For instance, broccoli, cauliflower, carrots and even potatoes retain their colour, shape, 'biting' texture and flavour – all the qualities that used to end up in the water they were boiled in.

Sauté This method is often crucial in order to bring out the aroma and flavour of onions, garlic and some vegetables. However, we recommend a distinct form of sauté to help you keep your fat intake to a minimum.

The New Sauté method does not use oil but still achieves the flavour, aroma, texture and nutritional quality desired from the sauté stage of cooking. Instead of oil, a very small amount (usually 2 fl oz/60ml) of liquid is heated in the pan until it bubbles furiously. The liquid may be water, stock, tomato juice, vinegar, gravy broth, dilute yeast extract or, indeed, any liquid you wish to use. Once the liquid is heated, the food is added and stirred constantly over a medium to high heat. As the food is more likely to stick in this method, the sauté time is not so long and the heat is slightly higher than in an oil sauté.

Frying Fried food is not recommended.

Boiling Rice and beans may be boiled and some sauces and soups may be brought to a boil before reducing them to a simmer. However, boiling is not used to cook vegetables as it greatly reduces their nutritional value and may cause them to lose texture, colour and flavour.

Grilling This method of cooking greatly reduces or eliminates the use of oil and fat in cooking.

Raw Most of the foods you will eat may be eaten raw. With a few exceptions (such as cooked carrot), raw food is nutritionally richer than its cooked counterpart and often has much more flavour. Buy organically grown foods when possible, especially fruits and vegetables. Raw foods are opportunities for you to create visual interest in your meal according to how you slice, shred, tear and chop them. And because they can be very colourful, you may wish to bring out the artist in you and serve them in dishes of unusual shapes and colours.

Cooking Beans

Most beans double in bulk once they are cooked. To gauge how much you need for a meal, the rule of thumb is that 55-115g (2-4 oz) of dried beans are enough for one serving, depending on what will accompany them. All beans must be well washed and well cooked to avoid indigestion.

Measure the beans into a mixing bowl and pick them over to remove any stones or unwanted pieces of bean.

Cover the beans with cold water and wash them very well by swirling your hand through them and exerting a scrubbing motion. Pour the water away and repeat this process three times, or until the water is clear. Drain the beans.

Cover the beans with water and leave them to soak overnight or all day while you are at work. Soaking the beans helps to prevent the flatulence that some people suffer from eating beans.

Drain the beans and throw the water away. Tip the beans into an iron pot, sprinkle 1 teaspoon salt over them and cover them with water. Bring them to the boil and boil rapidly for ten minutes, then simmer with the pan partially covered for 1-3 hours, depending on the type of bean you are cooking. The beans must remain covered in water and they must cook until they are easily squashed between your tongue and the top of your mouth. If they are undercooked you will get a stomach ache.

Alternatively, most beans may be pressure cooked. Cover the beans with water, cover the cooker and bring up to pressure. Cook at pressure for 20-40 minutes, depending on the type of bean you are cooking. (Please refer to the leaflet accompanying your pressure cooker or use the suggested times listed below.)

Red lentils and split peas do not require soaking or pressure cooking. In fact, they can clog up the valve of a pressure cooker and you may prefer to cook them in a pan. The red lentils are especially quick to cook and are very useful for a quick, nutritious meal.

Cooking Times

Chickpeas: Soak overnight. Cook for 30 minutes in the pressure cooker; 3 hours in the pot.

Kidney Beans: Soak overnight. Cook for 30 minutes in the pressure cooker; 1½ hours in the pot.

Butter Beans: Soak for 4-6 hours. Cook for 30 minutes in the pressure cooker; 1½ hours in the pot.

Soy Beans: Soak overnight. Cook for 40 minutes in the pressure cooker; at least 3 hours in the pot.

Black-Eyed Beans: Soak 4-6 hours. Cook for 20 minutes in the pressure cooker; 1 hour in the pot.

Lentils and Split Peas: Wash them well. Cook for 20 minutes in the pressure cooker; 1 hour in the pot.

5. WHERE TO FIND YOUR VITAMINS AND MINERALS

Vitamin A	Yellow and dark-green fruits and vegetables.
Vitamin B	Yeast, whole grains, legumes, nuts, molasses, dark-green leafy vegetables, root vegetables, soy beans, peanuts, sesame seeds, sunflower seeds, pumpkin seeds, wheat germ, Plamil® soya milk.
Vitamin C	Citrus fruits, rose hips, melon, strawberries, tomatoes, sprouted alfalfa, green peppers, broccoli.
Vitamin D	Fortified foods, including Plamil® soya milk, sunshine.
Vitamin E	Whole grains, molasses, dark-green leafy vegetables, sweet potatoes.
Calcium	Dark-green leafy vegetables, molasses, legumes, almonds.
Iron	Dark-green leafy vegetables, molasses, dried fruits, fermented soy bean products.
Magnesium	Whole grains, molasses, nuts, dark-green leafy vegetables.
Phosphorus	Nuts, whole grains, legumes.
Potassium	Whole grains, dried fruits, legumes, fresh vegetables, sunflower seeds.
Zinc	Mushrooms, soy beans and soy bean products, yeast, pumpkin seeds, sunflower seeds.

6. ARE YOU OVERWEIGHT?

The following charts are drawn from the figures compiled by the Metropolitan Life Insurance Company of New York, and give the approximate upper and lower limits to weight for each category of height, frame and gender.

Desirable Weights for Men and Women Aged 25 and Over

MEN: wearing indoor clothing and shoes with one-inch heels.

Height cm/inches	Small Frame kg/lbs	Medium Frame kg/lbs	Large Frame kg/lbs
157/5' 2"	51-54/112-120	53-58/118-129	57-64/126-141
160/5' 3"	52-56/115-123	55-60/121-133	58-65/129-144
162/5' 4"	53-57/118-126	56-62/124-136	60-67/132-148
165/5' 5"	55-58/121-129	58-63/127-139	61-69/135-152
167/5' 6"	56-60/124-133	59-65/130-143	63-71/138-156
170/5' 7"	58-62/128-137	61-67/134-147	64-73/142-161
173/5' 8"	60-64/132-141	63-69/138-152	66-75/147-166
175/5' 9"	62-66/136-145	64-71/142-156	68-77/151-170
178/5' 10"	64-68/140-150	66-73/146-160	70-79/155-174
180/5' 11"	65-70/144-154	68-75/150-165	72-81/159-179
183/6' 0"	67-72/148-158	70-77/154-170	74-83/164-184
185/6' 1"	69-74/152-162	72-79/158-175	76-86/168-189
188/6' 2"	71-76/156-167	74-82/162-180	78-88/173-194
190/6' 3"	73-78/160-171	76-84/167-185	81-90/178-199
193/6' 4"	74-79/164-175	78-86/172-190	83-93/182-204

WOMEN: wearing indoor clothing and shoes with two-inch heels.

Height cm/inches	Small Frame kg/lbs	Medium Frame kg/lbs	Large Frame kg/lbs
147/4' 10″	42-44/92-98	44-49/96-107	47-54/104-119
150/4' 11″	43-46/94-101	45-50/98-110	48-55/106-122
152/5' 0″	44-47/96-104	46-51/101-113	49-57/109-125
155/5' 1″	45-49/99-107	47-53/104-116	51-58/112-128
157/5' 2″	46-50/102-110	49-54/107-119	52-59/115-131
160/5' 3″	48-51/105-113	50-55/110-122	53-61/118-134
162/5' 4″	49-53/108-116	51-57/113-126	55-63/121-138
165/5' 5″	50-54/111-119	53-59/116-130	57-64/125-142
167/5' 6″	52-56/114-123	54-61/120-135	58-66/129-146
170/5' 7″	53-58/118-127	56-63/124-139	60-68/133-150
173/5' 8″	55-59/122-131	58-65/128-143	62-70/137-154
175/5' 9″	57-61/126-135	60-67/132-147	64-72/141-158
178/5' 10″	59-64/130-140	62-68/136-151	66-74/145-163
180/5' 11″	61-65/134-144	64-70/140-155	68-76/149-168
183/6' 0″	63-67/138-148	65-72/144-159	69-78/153-173

Note: for each year under 25, women between the ages of 18 and 24 should subtract 1 lb (455g) from the upper limit of their 'category'. Weight measured in the nude may be 2-5 lb (1-2.25 kg) less than that measured in indoor clothing.

7. FURTHER READING

Exercise for the Over-50s, Dr Russell Gibbs, Jill Norman Ltd, London, 1981.

High Energy Living, Caroline Laporte, Century Hutchinson, London, 1988.

Relaxation East and West: A Manual of Poised Living, James Hewitt, Rider, London, 1982.

The Caring Cook, Janet Hunt, Vegan Society Publications, 1987.

The Farm Vegetarian Cookbook, Ed. Louise Hagler, The Book Publishing Company, 1978.

Vegan Nutrition, Dr Michael A. Klaper, Vegan Society Publications, Oxford, 1988.

Vegan Nutrition, Dr Gill Langley, Vegan Society Publications, Oxford, 1988.

Why You Don't Need Meat, Peter Cox, Thorsons Publishers Ltd, Wellingborough, 1986.

8. USEFUL ADDRESSES

Action on Smoking and Health (ASH), 5-11 Mortimer Street, London W1N 7RJ. Telephone: 01-637 9843.

Autogenic Training, 101 Harley Street, London W1N 1DF. Telephone: 01-935 1811.

British Cardiac Society, 7 St Andrew's Place, London NW1. Telephone: 01-486 6430.

British Heart Foundation, 102 Gloucester Place, London W1H 4DH. Telephone: 01-953 0185. NOTE: There are eleven regional offices for the BHF. Please look in your phone directory for that nearest to you.

British Holistic Medical Association, 179 Gloucester Place, London NW1 6DX. Telephone: 01-262 5299.

British Wheel of Yoga, 80 Leckhampton Road, Cheltenham, Gloucestershire GL53 0BN.

The Coronary Artery Disease Research Association (CORDA), Tavistock House North, Tavistock Square, London WC1H 9TH. Telephone: 01-387 9779.

Coronary Prevention Group, 60 Great Ormond Street, London WC1N 3HR. Telephone: 01-833 3687.

Coronary Prevention in Children Project, Exeter Health Authority, Exeter.

Greater London Alcohol Advisory Service (GLAAS), 146 Queen Victoria Street, London EC4V 4BX. Telephone: 01-248 8406.

The Health Education Authority, Mabledon Place, London WC1. Telephone: 01-631 0930.

The Keep-Fit Association, National Secretary, 16 Upper Woburn Place, London WC1H 0QG. Telephone: 01-387 4349.

Northern Ireland ASH, c/o The Ulster Cancer Foundation, 40 Eglantine Avenue, Belfast BT9 6DX.

Northern Ireland Coronary Prevention Group, Bryson House, 28 Bedford Street, Belfast BT2 7FJ.

Relaxation for Living, 29 Burwood Park Road, Walton-on-Thames, Surrey KT12 5LH. Telephone: 093-22 27826.

Scottish ASH, Royal College of Physicians, 9 Queen's Street, Edinburgh EH2 1JQ.

Scottish Health Education Group, Health Education Centre, Woodburn House, Canaan Lane, Edinburgh EH10 4SG.

Society of Teachers of the Alexander Technique, 10 London House, 266 Fulham Road, London SW10 9EL. Telephone 01-351 0828.

The Vegan Society, 33-35 George Street, Oxford OX1 2AY. Telephone: 0865-722166.

The Women's League of Health and Beauty, 18 Charing Cross Road, London WC2 0HR. Telephone: 01-240 8456.

NOTE: The following organizations each have regional offices, please look in your phone book for that nearest to you. Ring or write for advice on first-aid courses that may help you save the life of someone having a heart attack.

Ambu International, Head Office, Charlton Road, Midsomer Norton, Bath BA3 4DR.

The British Red Cross Society, Head Office, 9 Grosvenor Crescent, London SW1X 7EJ.

The Royal Life-Saving Society, Head Office, Mountbatten House, Studley, Warwickshire.

St Andrew's Ambulance Association, Head Office, Milton Street, Glasgow G4 0HR.

St John's Ambulance, Head Office, 1 Grosvenor Crescent, London SW1X 7EF. Telephone: 01-235 5321.

9. SUPPLIERS

Beta Fibre supplied by: British Sugar plc, Industrial Sales Dept., PO Box 26, Oundle Road, Peterborough, PE2 9QU. Telephone: 0733-63171.

Biosalt^{TM} Biochemically balanced mineral salt compound supplied by: Gilbert's Health Foods Ltd, Marfleet, Kingston-upon-Hull, HU9 5NJ.

Cantamega 2000 vitamin and mineral supplement supplied by: G & G Food Supplies Ltd, 175 London Road, East Grinstead RH19 1YY. Telephone: 0342-312811; Larkhall Laboratories plc, 225-229 Putney Bridge Road, London SW15 2PY. Telephone: 01-874 1130.

Comvita Unsalted Food Yeast supplied by: New Zealand Natural Food Importers, 9 Holt Close, Highgate Wood, London N10 3HW. Telephone: 01-444 5660.

Engevita Nutritional Yeast Flakes supplied by: Marigold Health Foods Ltd, Unit 10, St Pancras Commercial Centre, 63 Pratt Street, London NW1 0BY. Telephone: 01-267 7368.

Oat Bran supplied by: Quaker Oats Ltd, PO Box 24, Bridge Road, Southall, Middlesex, UB2 4AG. Telephone 01-574 2388.

NOTE: Conversion to mmols/litre
Sometimes you will find cholesterol measured in milligrams per decilitre (abbreviated to mg/dL). These values can be converted to millimoles (mmols) by dividing by 38.66.

FURTHER INFORMATION
The information contained in this book is regularly updated in *The Whole Family Newsletter,* produced by Peter Cox and Peggy Brusseau. If you would like to receive information about it, or would like to write to them, please send a large stamped self-addressed envelope to:

The Whole Family Newsletter,
PO Box 1612,
London NW3 1TD

REFERENCE NOTES

1 *Daily Telegraph,* 5 August 1988
2 *The Health Scandal,* Vernon Coleman, Sidgwick & Jackson Ltd, 1988
3 Ibid
4 *Guardian,* 23 November 1988
5 Survey of Pharmaceuticals, *Financial Times,* 8 November 1988
6 *Guardian,* 23 November 1988
7 'Cutting into cholesterol. Cost-effective alternatives for treating hypercholesterolemia', Kinosian, B.P.; Eisenberg, J. M., Department of Medicine, University of Maryland, Baltimore. *JAMA,* 15 April 1988, 259 (15) pps2249-54
8 Adapted from guidelines issued by the US National Heart, Lung and Blood Institute
9 Adapted from 'A scoring system to identify men at high risk of a heart attack', Shaper, A. G. et al, *Health Trends,* 1987, Vol. 19
10 'Regression and progression of early femoral atherosclerosis entreated hyperlipoproteinemic patients', Barndt, R.; Blankenhorn, D. H. and Crawford, D. W. *Annals of internal medicine,* 86, 139-146
11 *JAMA,* 19 June 1987
12 *JAMA,* August 1988
13 Committee on Medical Aspects of Food Policy, Report of the Panel on Diet in Relation to Cardiovascular Disease, 1984
14 Report by the Coronary Prevention Group (UK), 26 May 1987
15 *Guardian,* 24 July 1984
16 Report by the National Advisory Committee on Nutritional Education (NACNE), 1983; also Prevention of Coronary Heart Disease, Report by the Expert Committee of the World Health Organization, Geneva, 1982, (Technical Report Series, No. 678); The Surgeon General's Report on Nutrition and Health, US Department of Health and Human Services, 1988, including recommendations from the American Heart Association and the American Cancer Society.
17 Committee on Medical Aspects of Food Policy. Report of the Panel on Diet in Relation to Cardiovascular Disease, 1984
18 Dr Millicent Higgins, US National Heart, Lung and Blood Institute, as reported in *The Times,* 11 February 1988 and 24 November 1988
19 *Financial Times,* 29 October 1988
20 Dr Lars Ekeland, University of North Carolina at Chapel Hill, *New England Journal of Medicine,* 15 November 1988
21 'Women's Health Today', Office of Health Economics, 23 November 1987
22 Dr Lars Ekeland, op. cit.
23 Dr John Betteridge, medical adviser to the Family Heart

Association, quoted in *Today,* 11 August 1988

24 *The Quick Cholesterol and Fat Counter,* Peter Cox and Peggy
Brusseau, Century Hutchinson, 1989

25 'Plasma lipids and lipoprotein cholesterol concentrations in people
with different diets in Britain', Thorogood, M; Carter, R; Benfield,
L.; McPherson, K.; Mann, Jl. *Br Med J* [Clin Res], 8 August 1987,
295 (6594) pp 351-3

26 For more details about healthy eating without meat, see *Why You
Don't Need Meat,* Peter Cox, Thorsons, 1986

27 'Effects of Dietary Fish Oil on Serum Lipids and Blood Coagulation
in Peritoneal Dialysis Patients', Lempert, K. D. et al. *Am. J. Kid.
Dis.,* 11: 170-175, February 1988

28 'Effects of a fish oil concentrate in patients with
hypercholesterolemia', Demke, D. M.; Peters, G. R.; Linet, O. I.;
Metzler, C. M.; Klott, K. A.; *Atherosclerosis,* 70, 1988, 73-80

29 'Adverse effect of omega-3 fatty acids in non-insulin-dependent
diabetes mellitus', Glauber, H.; Wallace, P.; Griver, K; Brcchtel, G.
Annals of Internal Medicine, 1988: 108:663-668

30 'Direct and indirect effects of dietary fibre on plasma lipoproteins in
man', Katan, M. B. *Scand J. Gastroenterol* [Suppl], 1987

31 'Effects of an oats fibre tablet and wheat bran in healthy volunteers',
Vorster, H. H.; Lotter, A. P; Odendaal, I. *S Afr Med J,* 29 March
1986

32 'Hypocholesterolemic effects of oat-bran or bean intake for
hypercholesterolemic men', Anderson, J. W.; Story, L.; Sieling, B.;
Chen, W. J.; Petro, M. S.; Story, J. *American Journal Of Clinical
Nutrition,* December 1984

33 'Oat-bran intake selectively lowers serum low-density lipoprotein
cholesterol concentrations of hypercholesterolemic men', Kirby, R.
W.; Anderson, J. W.; Sieling, B.; Rees, E. D.; Chen, W. J.; Miller, R.
E.; Kay, R. M. *American Journal Of Clinical Nutrition,* May 1981

34 'Serum lipid response to a fat-modified, oatmeal-enhanced diet', Van
Horn, L.; Emidy, L. A.; Liu, K. A.; Liao, Y. L.; Ballew, C.; King, J.;
Stamler, J. *Prev Med,* May 1988

35 *UPI,* 17 March 1988

36 'Effectiveness of individualized long-term therapy with niacin and
probucol in reduction of serum cholesterol', Cohen, L.; Morgan, J.
J Fam Pract, February 1988

37 'Dietary fiber content of selected foods', Anderson, J. W.; Bridges, S.
R. *American Journal Of Clinical Nutrition,* March 1988

38 'Hypocholesterolemic effects of oat and bean products', Anderson, J.
W. and Gustafson, N.J. *American Journal Of Clinical Nutrition,*
September 1988

39 *The Times,* 8 February 1988

40 'Effects of solid and liquid guar gum on plasma cholestrol and

triglyceride concentrations in moderate hypercholesterolemia', Superko, H. R.; Haskell, W. L.; Sawrey-Kubicek, L.; Farquhar, J. W. *Am J Cardiol,* 1 July 1988

41 'Dietary fiber in management of diabetes', Vinik, A. I.; Jenkins, D. J. *Diabetes Care,* February 1988

42 'Effects of guar gum in male subjects with hypercholesterolemia', Aro, A,; Uusitupa, M.; Voutilainen, E.; Korhonen, T. *American Journal Of Clinical Nutrition,* June 1984

43 'A double-blind evaluation of guar gum in patients with dyslipidaemia', Tuomilehto, J.; Karttunen, P.; Vinni, S.; Kostiainen, E.; Uusitupa, M. *Hum Nutr Clin Nutr,* March 1983

44 'Long-term treatment of hypercholesterolemia with a new palatable formulation of guar gum', Simons, L. A.; Gayst, S.; Balasubramaniam, S.; Ruys, J. *Atherosclerosis,* October 1982

45 'Cholestyramine plus pectin in treatment of patients with familial hypercholesterolemia', Schwandt, P.; Richter, W. O.; Weisweiler, P.; Neureuther, G. *Atherosclerosis,* September 1982

46 'Natural hypocholesterolemic agent: pectin plus ascorbic acid', Ginter, E.; Kubec, F. J.; Vozar, J.; Bobek, P. *Int J Vitam Nutr Res,* 1979

47 'Cholesterol-lowering effects of psyllium hydrophilic mucilloid for hypercholesterolemic men', Anderson, J. W.; Zettwoch, N.; Feldman, T.; Tietyen-Clark, J.; Oeltgen, P.; Bishop, C. W. *Arch Intern Med,* February 1988

48 'Influence of a psyllium-based fibre preparation on faecal and serum parameters', Burton, R.; Manninen, V. *Acta Med Scand* [Suppl], 1982

49 'Anaphylaxis following psyllium ingestion', Zaloga, G. P.; Hierlwimmer, U. R.; Engler, R. J. *J Allergy Clin Immunol,* July 1984

50 'Anaphylactic shock due to ingestion of psyllium laxative', Suhonen, R.; Kantola, I.; Bjorksten, F. *Allergy,* July 1983

51 'Olive-oil-enriched diet: effect on serum lipoprotein levels and biliary cholesterol saturation', Baggio, G.; Pagnan, A.; Muraca, M.; Martini, S.; Opportuno, A.; Bonanome, A.; Ambrosio, G. B.; Ferrari, S.; Guarini, P.; Piccolo, D. et al. *American Journal of Clinical Nutrition,* June 1988

52 'Effect of monounsaturated fatty acids versus complex carbohydrates on high-density lipoproteins in healthy men and women', Mensink, R. P.; Katan, M. B. *Lancet,* 17 January 1987

53 US Department of Agriculture, Science and Education Administration, Agriculture Handbook, No. 8-4, 1979

54 *The Quick Cholesterol and Fat Counter,* Peter Cox and Peggy Brusseau, Century Hutchinson, 1989